HELL IS NOT FOR ANGELS

HELL IS NOT FOR ANGELS

Rough Justice Follows Biker's Code of Silence

by

Stephen D. Smith

edited by

Alan Twiddle

Twiddlesmith Publishing Ltd
1997

First published in Great Britain in 1997
by Twiddlesmith Publishing Limited,
Whitton House,
11 York Road
Beverley
East Yorkshire
HU17 8DP

A CIP record for this book is available from the British Library

ISBN
ISBN 1 901853 05 5 Hardback Edition
ISBN 1 901853 00 4 Paperback Edition

Printed in Great Britain by Redwood Books Limited,
Trowbridge, Wilts.

Dedication

I would like to dedicate this, my first book, to the memory of my father, Douglas and my brother Neville, neither of whom lived to see it published.

THE AUTHOR WOULD LIKE TO THANK THE FOLLOWING:

Saveiro Aversa & Lorraine, Keith Borer Consultants, Barbara Bramall, Lynne and Bob Ego, Dr. Robert Evans, Bernard Ewart, Jonathan Ford, Alan R. Goldsack Q.C., Christine Goldsack, Ian Goldsack, Christopher Good, Andrew Hatton, Mattie Hawkins, Charles Hunter, Michael Jarvis, Rebecca Joynes, Elaine Jubb, Alison Keys, Peter Large, David Lidster, John Megson, Sharon Megson, Shaun Megson, Stella Megson, Sylvia Menzies, Irene McMillan, Tim Norburn, Karen Price, Len Pygot, Margaret Renn, Kate Smith, Robert C. Smith, John Tee, Stephen Thomas, John Thompson, Bill Townsend, Max Twoey, Alan Twiddle, John Ware, Paul Watson, Paul Wilkinson, Roni Wilkinson, Newton Wright and of course . . . Albert.

Contents

Foreword

Friday 13th June 1990. 6.30pm.

I was in Armley jail trying to convince the hospital wing prison officer that the last thing that I wanted was to begin a life sentence for murder by spending time under observation in the prison hospital.

Less than three hours earlier I had been convicted of the murder, by stabbing, of Stephen Rowley at Scarborough Mere on 23rd April 1989. Having been on remand for fourteen months in some of the worst jails in England, I was about to start a life sentence for a crime I had not committed.

Unlike many people who have been wrongly imprisoned, I was as much to blame as anyone else. As a member of the Druids motorcycle group, I merely kept the *code* believing that if I was wrongly convicted the murderer would step forward. I now realize that I was naive to think that loyalty to the group could be placed before freedom, At the time I truly believed that the real murderer would come forward or at least be shamed into coming forward by the rest of the group.

Within a week of my conviction I was working on an appeal but my solicitors who had represented me during the trial had advised me that without new evidence there was little chance of an appeal being granted.

Thinking that they had lost interest in my case I contacted many other solicitors throughout the country but after showing some initial concern they all apologised for the fact that without legal aid being granted they would be unable to work on my behalf. I could not blame them as nobody in his right mind would work for nothing.

This is where Steve Smith came in. My father Shaun was my only regular visitor and when he threatened to stop coming unless I told him the name of the real murderer, I finally gave in, at which point he mentioned Steve, telling me that he would try and get him to visit me.

I held out little hope, but sometime later Steve came to see me. He was down to earth, pulled no punches and always told me exactly what he thought, whether I liked it or not. I liked him and found conversation easy, but with no new evidence the situation was the same as the one the other solicitors had found.

But Steve was different. He believed I was innocent of murder, and he would not let me rot in prison knowing that an injustice had been done. He worked on my case for over a year before legal aid was finally granted, when he presented vital new evidence that had been given by Stella Harris.

Stella had been at Scarborough Mere on the night of the murder and she had witnessed the stabbing. She was prepared to make a statement and give evidence in court, but one of the hardest things that I have ever done was to let her do it. On two occasions I asked her not to get involved as I knew what the Druids were capable of.

However, I only agreed when I was assured that everything would be done to guarantee her safety.

My concern was justified, but she proved that she had more balls than the lot of them. Not bad for a woman of 4' 11"!

The fight for my freedom taught me to trust and believe in people again: in a woman who put her very life at risk to right a wrong done to a friend, and in a man who put his reputation and wallet on the line for justice.

John Megson
April 1997

Introduction

I decided to write a book about the John Megson case, plainly and simply because John himself asked me to.

It is, in my view, a wonderful story. It has tension, disappointment, success and, most of all, a happy ending – especially for his family who went through thick and thin until the case was won.

My involvement started in 1991 when Shaun Megson approached me with his theory concerning his son John's conviction for murder. Incredible as it seemed at the time, here was a man with no legal qualifications who presented a well structured argument, pointing out how the system had got it wrong. The system didn't believe him and, in the beginning, neither did I.

I had invested almost thirty years in the legal profession, having started as an office boy in the 60's and progressed to qualify as a legal executive and finally to become a solicitor of the Supreme Court. I thought that I was well versed in the morals of the criminal classes, but perhaps I had become a little blasé. I had fallen into the all too common trap of believing that I had seen it all. The job had turned me into a cynic and I believed that I could see all the old traditions falling by the wayside. I felt a *wind of change* blowing down the back of my neck and I was thinking of ways to take my leave of the profession I had loved.

The legal aid system as I knew it was under threat from a Government that seemed to be cutting corners to limit public spending in this area. The result of this action was inevitable and miscarriages of justice were bound to increase.

I had seen some of the most talented and responsible advocates begin to lose heart because of the enforced presence of a régime which was more concerned with limiting spending than with protecting the principles enshrined in the world renowned legal system in which I had grown up. Shaun Megson's reasoned argument made me consider whether there could have been a miscarriage of British Justice in his son's case.

If Shaun was to be believed, a High Court judge, a number of eminent Q.C.s and barristers, solicitors for the defence, the North Yorkshire Police, the Crown Prosecution Service and a jury of twelve people had all got it wrong. I thought that Mr Megson was talking through his hat and with as much politeness as I could muster, I told him so.

The case had been given to a firm of solicitors, who had replaced the ones who had prepared Megsons' original defence. However, they had made no progress towards a possible appeal, so why should I get involved in this particular case? I was reasonably successful and had as good a legal aid practice as is possible today. I wasn't short of work and if I put in twelve hours a day, six days a week I could pay the bills and enjoy the odd bottle of wine at weekends. There was no room for lost causes or *freebie work*. The offer of a case with no hope, no pay and nothing at the end of it was as welcome as a haemorrhoids operation. I have had to sit and wonder what it was that attracted me to this case and on reflection I believe it was the hopelessness of John Megson's situation that intrigued me. Why should Shaun Megson have such an obsession with his son's innocence? I even thought at one stage that if I kept my head down he might go away. He didn't. He became something of a nuisance and finally, I had to consider whether there might be something in what he had to say.

I was finally convinced that I should go and see John, when I was told that Shaun was trying to sell his stereo system in order to finance my visit. This left me with no alternative. I made the visit and Shaun kept his stereo.

Essentially, I went to Wakefield Prison, to tell John that he had no chance of an appeal and that he was wasting everyone's time. I expected the usual self pity and ego enhancing compliments, which are common when defendants want something from you. However, this man was different. Despite his prison setting he was dignified and articulate and did not ask for any favours.

We discussed his case for more than an hour and I was struck by his general demeanour which did not match that of any murderer I had ever dealt with. We finished our meeting by agreeing that there was little that I could do. However, we parted on excellent terms and I must confess that I was impressed by this affable young man.

I drove back to the office where I was met by Peter and Karen, my two advocate partners, who asked me about the consultation. I told them that the case troubled me because within five minutes of meeting him I knew that he was not a man who had committed murder. From that moment, I was hooked and the same obsession that was consuming Shaun Megson began to affect me. What happened over the next three years sustained my belief in a profession, which had begun to disappoint me. A solicitor may get one case in his whole career which stands out, but there are no guarantees of even one. Throughout my years in the job I had waited for the *big one*. It is true that I have had some very important cases, including a number of murder trials. Notably, I had dealt with the Arkwright murders, a multiple murder case involving four deceased, the content of which had surpassed all others in its horrifying detail but the Megson case was different.

This man dominated three years of my working life and became the case which troubled me more than any other because I knew that John Megson was innocent of murder. It was a case that I could not afford to lose because if I had, I would have been party to an injustice.

Hell is not for Angels shows how we set about proving our point. It tells of all the problems we encountered and the agonies we endured. I examine my dealings with the host of most interesting people that I met upon the way. I describe the incredible wall of silence which faced us at every stage and how we broke down that wall to the extent that even the doubters became persuaded.

In *Hell is not for Angels* I have tried to tell the story as it happened, showing the highs and lows and the incredible satisfaction that this case has given me over the years. I attempt to show in simple and non-legalistic language what it meant to me; the stress, the endeavour, the humour and the final victory. I try to describe that incredible moment when John arrived home and saw his father, who had supported him most, for the first time in five years outside prison walls. Such images are preserved lovingly in my mind.

My thanks go to Shaun Megson for his irrefutable belief in his son's innocence and to Stella, our star witness, for her courage and support without which we would not have had a case.

I thank Alan Goldsack Q.C., who, on his last case before becoming a judge, gave me wise help and advice which kept my feet firmly on the ground.

I also thank my partners and staff who put up with my dreadful stress induced mood swings and bad behaviour during the preparation of the case.

And last but by no means least, I thank John himself for his dignity and complete faith in the supporters who did so much to achieve his release.

Stephen D. Smith
May 1997

The Participants In The Case

THE DRUIDS

John Megson – MEX - Vice President
Colin McCombie – ANIMAL – Member
Adrian John Holmes – ADIE – Sergeant at Arms
Nicholas Woodhead – NICK – Member
Martin Foster – JUNKIE – Member
Brian Frankham – SNAKE – Treasurer
George Palmer – GEORDIE – Member
Simon Negrotti – YETTIE – Member
Robert Owen – BOGGY – Member
Lesley – Girlfriend of Brian Frankham
Stella Harris – Girlfriend of Robert Owen
Josephine – Girlfriend of Nicholas Woodhead
Kay Negrotti – Wife of Simon Negrotti

THE GEORDIES

Stephen Rowley – The Murder Victim
Neil Drakesmith – Friend of Stephen Rowley
Darren Lynn – Friend of Stephen Rowley who suffered stab wounds during the attack

Kevin Richardson – Friend of Stephen Rowley
Gary Foster – Friend of Stephen Rowley
Sharon Ross – Friend of Stephen Rowley

SECURITY GUARDS

Gary Metcalf & Geoffrey Smith	On duty at the Mere during the night of 21st/22nd April 1989.

THE POLICE DEALING WITH THE ENQUIRY

Detective Chief Superintendent George Chadwick – Head of Investigation
Detective Sergeant Andrew Bell – Interviewing Officer
Detective Constable George Lickes – Interviewing Officer
Detective Constable Ian Murray – Interviewing Officer

THE PROSECUTION

Martin Bethel QC – Original Counsel from the first trial
Guy Whitburn QC – Leading Counsel at the re-trial
Andrew Robertson – Junior Counsel throughout

THE DEFENCE TEAM

Roger Keen QC – Original Counsel during the first trial
Andrew Hatton – Junior Counsel during the first trial
Alan R Goldsack QC – Leading Counsel during the appeal hearing and the second trial

Paul Watson – Junior Counsel for the second trial
Karen A Price – Solicitor in defence team
Peter R Large – Solicitor in defence team
Stephen D Smith – Solicitor in defence team
Kate M Smith – Secretary to defence team
Doctor Robert Evans – Chemical pathologist – medical advisor to defence team
Keith Borer and Associates – Forensic scientists to the defence team

THE FAMILY

Shaun Megson – Father
Sharon Megson – Step-mother
Elaine Jubb – John Megson's girlfriend in April 1989
Derek Megson – John's brother
Julie Megson – John's sister

THE JUDICIARY

Mr Justice Potts QC – Judge at the original trial
Lord Justice Glidewell – Senior judge at the Court of Appeal hearing
Mr Justice McPherson of Clunny – Judge at the second trial

MEMBERS OF THE POLICE AT THE MURDER SCENE

Police Constable Richard O'Neal – First officer at scene
Police Constable Green – second officer at scene

THE MEDICAL TEAM

Geoffrey Leslie White – Leading ambulance man
Lewis Thompson – Ambulance man
Doctor Marianne Feinauer – House officer in general medicine at Scarborough Hospital
Doctor Hacki – Accident and emergency house doctor
Doctor Ghurye – Anaesthetist at Scarborough Hospital
Doctor Butte – Medical registrar at Scarborough in April 1989
Mr Ayres – Medical practitioner
Dr Denmark – Pathologist who carried out the post mortem on Rowley's body

THE BBC

Charles Hunter – Producer of the BBC *Rough Justice* programme
John Ware – Reporter
David Odd – Photographer
Howard Billingham – Editor
Irene McMillan – Researcher
Margaret Renn – Assistant producer
Elizabeth Clough – Executive producer
Nicholas Renton – Director

REGULAR CLIENT

Albert

I

The John Megson Case

Judicata res pro veritate accipitur
(A matter that has been adjudged is received as true)

"!!!!!!!!!! There are no toilet rolls in here Mr Smith!" bawled the agency cleaner.

It was 5.50pm. on 2 March, 1991, and I couldn't understand why she was picking on me. I was only the senior partner and of course the very least I could do was to organize the sanitary requirements for the office. I placated her by saying that someone would deal with the matter the following day. As I trudged upstairs, the cleaner's final words were ringing in my ears, "It's not very nice when there is no roll" she said.

"Of course not!', I replied imperiously, "It will be in my mind until the problem is resolved'. I announced this with an edge to my voice that came straight out of the famous book, *The Beginners Guide to Sarcasm Volume 2*.

It was one of those days I wanted to forget. It started badly and became systematically worse as the day went on. I reflected upon my career in the legal profession and

I came rapidly to the view that twenty-six years was enough for anyone to suffer and I began to wonder why on earth I had stayed in it for so long.

The profession was going through a period of change. The recession of the early 1990s was in full swing and solicitors who dealt with legal aid work were having their incomes cut to the bone by swingeing cuts to the legal aid purse. There was too much competition and if your clients didn't moan at you, your staff did, and if they didn't complain, the magistrates would. Whenever they left you alone, there was always the bank or the VAT men to squeeze the parts that other creditors could not reach.

I went into the tea room which had been equipped at great expense for our staff. Thinking that I would reflect on my day so far and check my messages over a large mug of tea, I found that all the milk had gone and the sugar bowl was empty. Disconsolately I climbed the three flights of stairs to my office. As I reached it, I noticed that some bright spark had tied a life-size monkey doll to the trunk of the plastic palm tree which *grows* outside my door . The monkey had a badge that read *Albert* the name of one of my most regular clients!

I had to complete a report of one of the cases I had dealt with that day involving a *ménage à trois*, although in Rotherham we call it the eternal triangle. This case involved my client who was a man who thought it was wrong to strike his children, but believed it perfectly normal to beat up his wife. He seemed to think that twenty-five years of marriage entitled him to certain rights and, having seen what he had done, I would have said lefts and uppercuts as well. The court had despatched him with a fine of £100 which was £50 less than the fine another client received on the same day in the same court for speeding.

I finished the report and then turned to the list of telephone messages that had accumulated on my desk. I selected a few that I felt I could deal with, one of which was from an old client called Shaun Megson. I had known Shaun for many years and always found him to be a dour Yorkshireman with a propensity for straight talking and a manner which exuded a blunt edge as wide as Ian Botham's bat. I had always been able to share a joke with him, so I decided to ring him back thinking that he might brighten up my day.

He answered the telephone and I realized immediately that he was not in a happy mood. He reminded me that he had a son called John who was in his early thirties, and although I had never met John, Shaun had often referred to him during our conversations in the past.

Shaun told me that John had been convicted of murder in May 1990 and jailed for life by Leeds Crown Court. He went on to say that his son was innocent and had been wrongly convicted, but had been told that an appeal was unlikely.

He was clearly very upset about what had taken place and I didn't know whether I was meant to agree with him, deny the proposition or just express regret. He had rung me to obtain a second opinion as to the prospect of an appeal because, although an appeal had been discussed, nothing more had happened. I thought that this was a case of a man who could not come to terms with the realization that his son was a convicted killer. I did not wish to upset him any further but I suggested that there must have been some evidence against John, otherwise the jury would not have found him guilty.

I believed that this was one problem for me which would go away, because as John had not instructed me in the trial, I couldn't see why he would want to instruct me now, particularly as I didn't know him. I was soon to find that I had underestimated Shaun's powers of persuasion.

I made a few more telephone calls before deciding to call it a day. As I walked to the car, I passed a local pub where all the local ne'er-do-wells tend to gather. Two such likely lads who had obviously been there all day, were standing outside hoping to see a friendly face to *tap* for a *sub. Subbing* is an art form in Rotherham, whereby down-and-outs impose themselves upon passers-by in order to obtain money on the pretext of having to pay off rent arrears to secure their accommodation. In reality, they use it to buy more beer.

One of them approached me and in as pleasant a fashion as he could, asked, "How's about a couple of pints then Smithy?"

"No thank you', said I, "I'm driving."

He was unable to deal with the speed of my repartee and I managed to escape with what little money I had. Arriving home, I found that there was no one in and I had left my house keys in the office. It certainly had been one of those days.

The following morning I was in the office early to catch up on the number of jobs I hadn't been able to face the day before. As soon as the switchboard opened a call came in from Shaun Megson who told me that within a matter of minutes he would be in the office with John's papers. "Delightful," I said, totally without enthusiasm as I put the phone down.

I leave for court as near to 9.30am as possible, and at 9.29am I set off, to be greeted in reception by Shaun Megson with the biggest wad of papers I had seen in a long time. I left them in reception and set off for a day in my beloved Rotherham Magistrates' Court.

It was a very good day. Indeed, it was one of those days when you don't seem to be able to put a foot wrong. I finished the morning session at about 1.10pm, collected my papers and got to the front of the sandwich queue before the major rush. I walked back to the office with the intention of clearing the morning's dictation to find two messages from Shaun Megson both asking if I had read the papers.

His persistence was almost annoying, and on the Friday of that week when he contacted me again, I told him that I would read the papers at the weekend without fail.

That afternoon I had a heavy list of cases, and so returned to court early. Albert, a member of a well known Rotherham family who had been extremely loyal to my firm over many years, was waiting to see me. Albert is one of eleven children and all but one of them have previous convictions. However the one who hadn't come to the attention of the court was only eight years old.

The case I was to deal with involved Albert being charged with stealing a car door. He had acquired a Ford Cortina Mk4, a model which was rather popular with the local criminal fraternity. Unfortunately, the front passenger door had been badly damaged and needed replacing. The usual stop-off point would have been the local vehicle dismantlers, but Albert did not have sufficient funds and so he decided that he would seek out an appropriate Ford, pinch a door and put it on his own car.

He had great difficulty tracking down a Cortina and so he finally stole a door from an Escort. Somehow, with the aid of welding tackle and a big hammer he made the Escort door fit. However, one afternoon, the local Maltby Police were driving around the little town centre when they spotted Albert's Mk4 Cortina. Their attention was immediately drawn to this vehicle because it was bright red, except for the passenger door which was green.

The police had a report about a stolen car door and it didn't take the skills of Poirot to connect this door to the theft.

They stopped the Cortina and promptly put their suspicions to Albert. "What makes you think its me, you wankers?" queried an aggrieved Albert.

"The colour of the door is a dead give away Albert", said one police officer. Albert shrugged his shoulders and announced,

"It's a fair cop," and followed the police car to Maltby police station where he promptly admitted the offence.

The police removed the door from the car and waited for the arrival of the owner much to Albert's annoyance as he had to drive home without any passenger door at all. How *could* the police do such a thing!?

He appeared at the court that day because a previous court had ordered a probation report, which was the practice when a fine or conditional discharge are thought to be inappropriate and a more serious penalty is called for. I was just going through the probation report with him before going into the court, when I noticed a reference to him being a surviving twin and I had to confess, that in all the years that I had known the family, I had not realized that Albert had a twin. I questioned him about this:

"I didn't know you had a twin Albert?" I asked.

"Argh," replied Albert with the restricted language for which he was famous.

"What was it?", I queried.

"A lad," replied Albert.

"I understand from the report that your twin died, but it doesn't say how old he was. How old was he?" I asked.

"Same age as me," replied Albert. There was nothing more to be said. We went into the court and Albert was followed by his entourage consisting of his wife, mother, various brothers and sisters and boozing friends. The court was rather amused by the circumstances surrounding the case and as a result I was able to minimize the seriousness of it somewhat by being jocular throughout my address to the magistrates.

Albert was ordered to do community service work, but before such an instruction can be given the defendant has to agree to the making of such an order. The magistrate who sentenced him asked the usual question,

"Are you prepared to carry out the requirements of this order?"

"Argh," replied Albert and the order was made.

I returned to the office that afternoon, presented a bunch of flowers to one of the typists who was leaving to have twins and ordered a drunk to leave the reception area for being obnoxious. As I walked to my office I wondered if our typist's twins would be the same age.

One day, about three weeks later, I returned from court to find a message from Shaun Megson. He had been away for a fortnight but was now back and wanting to know what I had made of the papers he had left with me.

I asked my secretary to make an appointment for Shaun and immediately transferred the papers from the top of my filing cabinet, where they had been gathering dust, to my desk where I started to read them.

The prosecution alleged that John Steven Megson was a member of a motor cycle gang, who as a group of bikers (as they prefer to be known) had travelled to Scarborough on the North Yorkshire coast on the 22nd day of April 1989, to watch the motor cycle racing on Oliver's Mount. This was a very popular annual event, attended by large groups of people travelling from all over the country.

One such group was a party of friends from the North East and included a young man called Stephen Rowley who was to lose his life that night at Scarborough Mere.

Rowley was not a biker, but enjoyed such events.

Both Rowley's and Megson's groups had chosen to camp by the edge of Scarborough Mere and during the evening they all consumed a large amount of alcohol. There appears to have been some shouting between the two groups with the result that the bikers from Sheffield who were known as the Druids, went to the Rowley encampment hell-bent upon trouble.

Rowley and another of his group called Darren Lynn were attacked. A number of bikers took part in the attack which ended with Rowley and Lynn being stabbed. Lynn, though badly injured, survived, but the nineteen year old Stephen Rowley died as a result of a wound to his heart. There was little evidence to connect any of the Druids to the killing, except for descriptions given by

Lynn and some of his friends to the effect that the assailants were from the biking fraternity.

The evidence in itself would have been insufficient to have secured a conviction, but in John's case, the police had seized his clothing after the incident and that clothing was found to have been stained with the blood of Stephen Rowley. John had denied having any contact with Rowley and so, when the forensic evidence was put to him, he had no explanation for it and indeed offered none. He simply could not explain how his clothing came to be stained with Rowley's blood.

There was, however, a further and more sinister reason for John to keep quiet. The Druids had a strict code of conduct, which included a rule that no one should make statements to the police. This rule was to become known as the Code of Silence and it was the observance of this which led to John's conviction for a murder he did not commit.

I had heard a little of these biking clubs but knew nothing of their strict codes of conduct and I could not understand why John had refused to give evidence in his own trial and in his own defence. He must have known that the jury would have been extremely suspicious about his silence and more importantly about why he refused to explain the presence of Rowley's blood on his clothing.

I was intrigued but little did I know that this case was to involve me in considerable newspaper attention and numerous interviews with the radio and television, to say nothing of two feature-length television programmes about the case. John was to become a cult figure among bikers throughout the country and I was to get ulcers, which persist to this day.

On the day of the meeting with Shaun, I had been called down to the police station because my loyal client Albert had been at it again. His mother, the ageing family matriarch, had existed on state benefit for most of her life and this had always prevented her from owning an automatic washing machine. Albert knew and regretted it.

That morning, Albert had been driving his Transit van in the town centre and had seen a large cardboard box bearing the name Hoover on the side panel. It stood outside a row of shops which included a branch of Currys, the electrical retailers. Albert pulled up his van alongside and with one of his brothers promptly loaded the box into the back, hoping not to be noticed.

Without inspecting his prize, he arrived at his mother's house, unloaded the booty and left it outside her front door.

Albert then rang the door bell and ran to hide behind the bus shelter on the opposite side of the road. He watched in horror as he observed his mother open the box and *become the proud owner of three thousand wire coat hangers.*

Unfortunately, one of the shop assistants at the dry cleaners next to Currys saw what had taken place, and had noted the registration number of Albert's van. The police had arrested him that afternoon and with considerable amusement, interviewed him. Albert realized that the evidence was overwhelming so with great reluctance, he agreed to admit the offence for which he was charged and bailed.

When I arrived back at the office, I found Shaun Megson waiting for me, I asked him to recount his son's story from beginning to end. His account of the case and particularly his explanation of John's involvement in the bikers' group, *The Druids*, fascinated me.

I believed that *Bikers* and *Hell's Angels* were the same and I have to admit that my image of them probably had been formed by TV re-runs of old films like *The Wild One* starring Marlon Brando as the leather clad leader of the *Black Rebels* motorcycle group.

Shaun soon put me right explaining that the *Hell's Angels* are only one group, albeit the most notorious and with a world-wide membership. To become a member a biker has to be initiated into the MCC (Motorcycle Club) and only then is entitled to wear the distinctive yellow *Hell's Angel* badge on their leathers. The MCC is still run from America with a London office. The largest British group is known as the *All England* chapter. However, a number of British groups did not want to be controlled by America and ignored the MCC.

The Druids was one of these groups and was set up in 1970 with its own membership hierarchy and appointed officers. At the time of the murder *The Druids* were made up as follows:

> **The President** is the leader of the group and is elected by the membership. As the title implies, the president holds a most important position, usually reserved for the individual with organizational skills and the respect of the other members. The President of *The Druids* at that time was a man known as Bandy (Ray Millward). Bikers are usually known by their nick-names and it is not unusual for people connected with the group not to know the real names of fellow members.

The Vice President is a senior position, again afforded to those who are respected within the group. The Vice President would act as senior member in the absence of the President. On 22nd April 1989 the Vice President was Mex (John Megson).

The Sergeant At Arms is a particular title reserved for the man who deals with the internal discipline within the group and sees to it that their behaviour falls within acceptable guidelines. On the fateful visit to Scarborough, The Sergeant At Arms was a man called Adie (Adrian Holmes) who was over six feet tall and well built.

The Secretary and **The Treasurer** are seen as minor roles within the hierarchy but can be stepping stones to the leadership. At the time of the trip, the Secretary was Snake (Brian Frankham), who by the time John Megson was released, would be President.

John had been involved in *The Druids* organization for some years having first joined it as a *Prospect*. A *Prospect* is, in effect, apprenticed to the other bikers, and at the beck and call of all members. However, John was soon made a full member and worked his way through the ranks, to become Sergeant At Arms and then Vice President.

The total membership of *The Druids* was about twenty. They held meetings on a fairly regular basis and as with many other *badge clubs* or *outlaw bikers*, as they were called, they had developed their own set of rules and regulations which had to be obeyed.

The rules were prominently displayed in the club

house in Fitzwilliam Road, Rotherham, South Yorkshire.

1. Patches – £20.00 a set.
2. Bike or Trike, 500c or over.
3. Bike must be in full working order between 1st April and 30th September.
4. The bike must be legally owned.
5. New Members will be on a three month probation period.
6. Patches to be flown at the member's discretion.
7. Members using drugs through injection will be severely dealt with and thrown out.
8. Members living outside Sheffield must phone at least twice a week.
9. No statements to be made to any police.
10. Voting on members, prospects etc, 75% in favour. President's vote must be in favour.
11. A member wanting to leave the club must give his reasons at a club meeting.
12. All club patches remain property of the club.
13. Any members wishing to become an honorary member must give their reasons at a club meeting.
14. Full members subs are £2.00 per week.
15. Property patches will only be worn by ol' ladies who have been with a full member for a minimum of three months if the club vote is in favour.
16. Fines: Late for meetings £3.00
    Absent £10.00
    Late for run £5.00
    Absent, fine to be the cost of the average amount of petrol used.

All rules are down to mitigating circumstances

Rule 9 became known as *The Code of Silence*, and it was John Megson's strict adherence to this rule that had led him to a life sentence for a murder his father was now telling me he had not committed.

John was in Wakefield Prison serving a life sentence for the murder of nineteen year old Stephen Rowley on 23rd April 1989. Rowley had been stabbed to death at a makeshift campsite around the edge of the mere in Scarborough, North Yorkshire, following the annual motor cycle races which take place on Olivers Mount overlooking the mere.

A large group of *The Druids* including a number of ol' ladies set out on the run to Scarborough with John, as Vice President, the senior member.

MEX –	John Megson (Vice President)
ADIE –	Adrian John Holmes (Sergeant At Arms)
SNAKE –	Brian Frankham (Secretary) accompanied by Lesley
ANIMAL –	Colin McCombie
BOGGY –	Robert Owen accompanied by Stella Harris
GEORDIE –	George Palmer
JUNKIE –	Martin Foster
NICK –	Nicholas Woodhead accompanied by Josephine
YETTIE –	Simon Negrotti accompanied by Helen

The next morning *The Druids* were arrested and interviwed by the police. John denied being present at the murder scene but particles of blood belonging to Rowley had been found on his clothing confirming that there had been contact between the two men. John was re-interviewed when the forensic evidence was available but instead of explaining what had happened, he chose to remain silent.

Shaun had taken over an hour to tell me his story and I realized how easy it had been for the jury to find John guilty. He had lied to the police and when his lie had been discovered he had refused to explain himself.

Now, three years later, it would be even more difficult to prove his innocence. Questions flooded into my head. Why had he refused to give evidence in his own defence? John had already seen three different firms of solicitors. If there had been a case for his defence, wouldn't they have noticed it?

"If you are right, an awful lot of people have got it wrong."

My words seemed to echo round the room. It was the first time I had spoken since Shaun began his story.

"They are wrong!" said Shaun passionately.

"But how do we prove it?" I asked.

"That's where you come in," said Shaun with a wry smile.

If John Megson had not stabbed Rowley, who had? I posed the question to Shaun not expecting an answer. However, I got one.

"Animal," said Shaun thoughtfully.

"Who?" I asked.

"Animal," replied Shaun.

"How do you know?" I asked.

"I managed to get it out of John," said Shaun, "but even then he wouldn't say it."

"I don't understand," I persisted.

"Well," continued Shaun, "he wouldn't tell me. He wouldn't tell anybody. So, week in week out I tried to wear him down but he wouldn't have it. Then, when the Druids stopped visiting him he started to wonder if he had been dumped. Weeks passed, months even and slowly but surely I got to him. If they had kept visiting him I wouldn't have stood a chance . . . but . . .," Shaun smiled before he continued.

"One day I thought . . . fuck it . . . he was going to tell me one way or another. I decided to tell him that if he didn't give me the name I would stop visiting him just like they had done. He would be on his own. That's worse than torture, fifteen years of that, and I meant it. It was a rotten day, raining as usual but when I got there I just told him."

I didn't speak I just nodded in encouragement.

"Then," continued Shaun, "I told him that I wanted to know or else he would be entirely alone. Even then he wouldn't speak it . . . we sat and looked at each other in silence . . . He said he couldn't say it . . . so I told him to write it down. He didn't want to but to keep up the pressure I passed him the first thing that came to hand. It was a bloody Kit-Kat wrapper . . . would you believe it? You could have cut the air with a knife . . . It was as if it was in slow motion. He picked up the pen . . . turned the wrapper over . . . then wrote . . . I tried to see what he was writing but it's hard to read when the words are upside down. When he finished I snatched it. It read *ANIMAL*, Colin McCombie."

Shaun had re-lived the scene in the visitors' room and it had drained him.

We both sat in silence while I took in the implications of what Shaun had said.

I was the first to speak.

"Well," I said, breaking the silence, "It's a start . . ."

II

The Beginning

I think that we
Shall never more, at any future time,
Delight our souls with talk of knightly deeds,
Walking about the gardens and the halls
Of Camelot, as the days that were.
Tennyson, Idylls of the King

John Megson was born on the 9th January, 1960 to Shaun and Betty Megson née Abrahams. As his parents had matrimonial difficulties, John was brought up by his maternal grandparents but had regular contact with his parents as they lived nearby. The marriage resulted in three children, John, Derek and Julie. After leaving the local junior school, with average grades John attended the Kimberworth Comprehensive School from 1971. In his third year he began playing truant to avoid English and Religious Studies. During this time he became interested in motorcycles and when not at school he spent much of his time riding and working on an old motorcycle which he and a friend had bought.

He never played truant on the days he had Maths, Physics or Engineering because these were his favourite subjects. The only difficulties he had at school were because he refused to wear school uniform and to stop smoking cigarettes. Despite the punishment meted out to him by the school, he would not wear the uniform and this refusal to conform moved with him into his adult life. He was keen enough on sport to play for the school rugby team, but this was the only sport that he ever had any real interest in. He passed all his CSE examinations with above average grades except in English and Religious Education.

When he left school at sixteen he was unemployed for about eight weeks, before opting for an engineering training course which he left in 1978 having been offered a job with the National Coal Board at Thurcroft Colliery. He began underground training and chose to go on a day-release scheme and night-school to study for a position as a colliery deputy. It was during this period that he met his first wife. He left the pit before he had completed his studies to be with this woman, as he was hopelessly infatuated with her. After about eight months of being unemployed, he realized that he was wasting his time and set out to find work.

He took a job at W.H. Booth Foundry as an assistant to the mechanic, servicing company cars and trucks. He decided to marry and opted for all the overtime he could get, doing extra jobs as a pattern maker, a moulder and even labouring. He was working seven days a week, usually from 6 am to 8 pm.

His son Stephen was born in October 1980 but due to the long hours he was working and with his free time taken up by motorcycles, his marriage failed. He also had a very serious road accident in which his best friend lost his right leg. John was seriously injured, damaging his leg and his left elbow.

He returned to live with his grandparents, taking only his clothes, tools and his motorcycles. His wife took the rest including their child whom he was to see only occasionally.

In April 1989, the only really serious conviction on his criminal record was a firearms offence which had been committed in 1985.

He had been on a run with one of his friends who had a shotgun which he normally kept as a wall decoration.

His friend had maintained the weapon and indeed had repaired it to the extent that it was capable of being fired. The two of them were heading for a motorcycle rally with the gun strapped to John's motorcycle when they were stopped by the police.

John admitted carrying the weapon. He was charged with possessing a firearm and sentenced to a term of six months' imprisonment of which he served four months.

This was an early indication that John was someone to whom his friends meant everything. He would even share the blame for offences they had committed and explained this by saying that they would have done exactly the same for him in a similar position. By the time he went to prison he had acquired a string of motoring convictions for such offences as having no licence, no insurance and no test certificate.

In 1985, he returned to Rotherham and to his family, meeting one of his old friends from the Druids who asked him to return to the group. It seemed that the club was more settled and the lawlessness that had been a trademark of the group had been phased out and so John agreed to become a *Prospect*.

He was well liked within the group and was found to

be a considerable diplomat, dealing with what he described as *dodgy situations* and keeping the lads in line. Everyone thought that he was good at this job and was greatly respected by the other members.

He then went on the *run* to Scarborough Mere.

On my initial perusal of the papers, I found that this was a very unfortunate case of a nineteen year old youth who was stabbed to death at Scarborough Mere in the early hours of 23rd April 1989. The Prosecution claimed that John Megson had done it and the jury agreed. John was convicted and sentenced to life imprisonment.

The judge appeared to have summed up the case properly and therefore I couldn't see any grounds for the prospects of a successful appeal. As there were no eye witnesses and as the police had found the deceased's blood on John Megson's clothes, there appeared to be nothing that could be done.

I arranged to see Shaun again with the rather unhappy task of telling him that he had no case. I tried to do so as nicely and with as much consideration for his feelings as I could. However, Shaun would have none of it. He was convinced that his son was innocent and after an hour, I was getting nowhere. "John kept his mouth shut and has not told the truth about what happened. He knows the identity of the real killer who has refused to come forward," pleaded Shaun.

The problem was that this was not a sufficient reason to appeal. "Even if that is true, it is not strong enough to force an appeal. If John knew that at the time of the trial, it cannot be classed as new evidence," I said forcefully. We agreed to differ on that point, but I was impressed with Shaun's forceful arguments and realized that he was not going to give in. I tried to find a way to get him out of my office, yet placate him at the same time.

"Will you just go and see him?" asked Shaun, "If you don't believe him or you think there is no case, then fair enough, but will you at least see him?"

The legal profession really does have to concentrate on the cases for which it is going to be paid and if it dealt with every query from all *would be* litigants without payment, the profession would be bankrupt within a week. However, I realized how much it meant to Shaun and I wanted to help if I could. I agreed that I would see John, but only when I was either in the area or visiting the prison. There was little likelihood of me visiting any other inmate in Wakefield Prison as it was a prison for men serving out sentences for convictions which had been fully dealt with including any appeals. After a fortnight, Shaun rang me again and asked me if there was any possibility of me visiting John the following week. He told me that he was trying to sell his stereo equipment to pay for the visit. At this point I gave in and agreed to see John free of charge.

I have to admit that my visit was under protest and I was annoyed at my own weakness in being persuaded to go. Nevertheless, I had not built up a practice by refusing to work or withholding a sympathetic word when it was necessary. I had lived by the maxim: *Cast thy bread upon the waters; for thou shalt find it after many days.* and the waterways of Rotherham had certainly been clogged with mine for years. Old habits die hard to quote yet another cliché and so, somewhat begrudgingly I set off for Wakefield.

I had worked there in the late sixties for my then mentor, George Towel, an ex-policeman who, at forty seven had qualified as a solicitor and formed his own practice. George taught me the rudiments of discipline in which, up to that time, I had been sadly lacking.

I walked through the high security doors of Wakefield Prison and signed the register before being subjected to the *ray-gun* which checks to see that no weapons are being carried into the prison. The security guard was satisfied that I had no Kalashnikovs or Bowie knives hidden on my person and I was allowed inside.

Today, due to the increasing problem of drugs in prisons many of Her Majesty's *hotels* demand that *special visits* such as solicitors, counsel and probation officers are also searched. This rather humiliating experience has now become normal practise in the prison service's fight against drugs.

Passing through two more security doors, I arrived in the visiting hall which was full of prisoners, their wives, girlfriends, parents, other relatives, friends and, as usual, hoardes of children who had quickly become bored with their monthly visit to fathers who were becoming strangers to them. The children were now rampaging around the visiting hall and the noise was deafening, with families having to shout to be heard even across the small prison tables.

I was fortunate enough to be taken to a small room off the main hall where I sat and waited for John to arrive.

While waiting, I couldn't help wondering what it must feel like to serve a sentence of life imprisonment when you are innocent of the crime. However, I still felt that there would be little I could do for John Megson.

I had only waited about five minutes when the door opened and in walked John. I was immediately aware of his size. He was six feet three inches tall with long black hair which had a few streaks of grey and he wore a long goatee beard. His appearance, including his extremely dark piercing eyes could be described as *Rasputinesque.*

We shook hands and I asked him to sit down. To ease the situation I offered him a cigarette which he readily accepted. We assessed each other rather like boxers before a fight. He was suspicious of me and obviously wondered why I had come when there was plainly nothing I could do.

To help him relax I suggested a cup of tea and got up to look for the WRVS kiosk. I returned with two cups and put one down in front of him. He had finished his cigarette and accepted another after some token resistance.

"Well," I said, finally getting down to business. "I don't think that there is a lot I can do. After all, the case is over and there appears to be no grounds for appeal that I can see."

I made my point forcefully because I am so used to vexatious litigants and whingeing defendants who cannot come to terms with a situation they themselves have created. I expected to face a barrage of complaints about solicitors, counsel, judges and juries because very few defendants are ever in prison for what they have done. It is almost always someone else's fault.

I was surprised at John's reaction.

"No offence, Mr Smith, but I didn't ask you to come. I'm seeing you because my father asked me to."

"Yes, of course but I didn't want to get off on the wrong foot," I said, knowing that I already had. "Tell me," I continued, "and please have another cigarette."

"No thanks," said John in an attempt to regain some lost dignity. "What do you want to know?"

"Well, what I really want to know is, who murdered Stephen Rowley?"

"I expect my Dad will have already told you," John continued. "It wasn't me at any rate."

"Your Dad is quite convinced that you are innocent."

"I am, but what of it?" said John, looking me straight in the eye. "But I don't think there is anything you can do about it."

His defiance gave way to defeatism and trailed off into silence.

"I'm quite prepared to try to help if I can," I said trying to re-establish myself in John's eyes.

"It's too late Mr Smith. The damage is done. Thank you for your interest. Perhaps you will tell my Dad that I saw you as he asked. It might persuade him to continue his visits."

John got up to leave offering me his hand. I took it with some reluctance as I did not want to leave on such a negative note. It was obvious that John was simply following his father's wishes and he had no other interest in seeing me. For a second I thought John might be preparing a *sting* to arouse my interest in his case but he had offered no *bait* at all. I realized that his only aim in agreeing to see me was to make sure that his father would continue to visit when all his *friends* seemed to have deserted him.

"Before you go," I asked, "tell me who murdered Rowley."

"Ask Dad," was his swift reply.

"I'm asking you," I countered.

"Look, thanks but no thanks. The situation is hopeless. I know I don't have any chance of an appeal. It's my fault and I can't see any way out. I know you mean well but if it's all the same to you . . ."

"At least have a cigarette before you go." I interrupted. "Please feel free. They are not mine. I don't smoke so I pinched them from someone back at the office."

For the first time I saw the shadow of a smile on John's face as he took another cigarette.

"I suppose the lighter is nicked as well?"

"Borrowed," I said, "from the same source."

John laughed for the first time and the sound echoed around my head. Unfortunately the lighter was empty so I left the interview room to *borrow* another. I found the officer in charge of visits.

"Could I pinch a lighter, please?" I asked.

"Who's it for?" he snapped back. "You?"

I was back at school. I panicked. "No. It's for an inmate."

"Let him get his own." the officer barked back.

I had almost turned sheepishly away when he spoke again. "Who is the prisoner?" he asked in a tone suggesting he was regretting his sharpness.

"Megson, 'A' wing."

"Oh," he said. "That's OK. Here, take my lighter. He's all right."

I was surprised that he had agreed so readily when he heard who the beneficiary was to be. "Is Megson all right then?" I asked.

"He's all right. We don't get any problems with him unless he gets problems himself," explained the jailer.

"Thank you," I said thinking that would be as close to a compliment this man would ever give a prisoner in his charge. I returned to the interview room and lit John's cigarette.

"I suppose your Dad is only trying to do his best for you, you know," I said looking for an answer.

For the first time John's shield dropped a little.

"I know he is. He means well. He's only doing what he thinks is best but I can't stand up in a court and say what happened even if I had a chance to get out. He doesn't understand that."

Knowing how Shaun felt, I thought that the least I could do was to put his point of view to John. "Shaun believes you to be innocent and so it is not surprising that he is doing what he can to help.

"Yes. I know I should have cooperated with him." He hesitated and then looked directly at me. "There is no prospect of re-opening the case, is there?"

It was my turn to hesitate. I didn't want to give him any false hope but I felt I could be completely honest with him. "You need some new evidence; someone who was there who will give evidence as to what they really saw. Surely one of them would be prepared to come forward."

John smiled a sardonic smile. "As I said earlier, I think we are wasting each other's time."

"Why?" I insisted.

"Would you put your neck in a noose if you had already avoided it? I don't think so." The cynical smile returned to his face. " I can't ask anyone to stick their neck out for me."

I had got him talking but as yet there were no real protestations of innocence, no accusatory outbursts and certainly no mention of the real killer. I had to know why.

"You didn't kill that lad did you?" I asked pointedly.

John thought for a moment. "Would it make any difference if I hadn't killed him?"

"Certainly," I replied energetically.

"But you still wouldn't be able to do anything would you?"

"Well no," I conceded. "But . . ."

"Well. There it is. What's the point?"

"Stand up and say who did it," I ordered.

"And then they will let me out will they? You and I know that won't happen and then what? Nothing. The code is breached for nothing and what do I have left?" He paused and I interjected.

"You mean that you are prepared to remain in prison for the rest of a life sentence for a murder you did not commit for some bloody stupid code that only you abide by? What sort of burke does that?"

"This one!" said John and then more quietly. "Yes, this one."

We both sat in silence looking at each other and waiting for the other to speak. I could think of nothing to say until; "Cigarette?" I asked calmly. John took one begrudgingly without speaking. "Very bad for your chest, smoking is," I said for want of something better to say. "You'll never run a marathon at this rate."

John looked at me for a second and then burst out laughing. It was infectious and I joined in but soon started to cough as I usually do when I laugh even though I had not smoked for over fifteen years.

"How many times round the exercise yard would that be?" John asked. He laughed while I coughed.

The laughter came to an end as I considered the hopelessness of his situation. We talked about anything but the case for a little while and this and the rapidly dwindling supply of cigarettes kept John with me until we were disturbed by the prison officer. "Five minutes please sir," he shouted through the open doorway.

"Well then," I said sitting upright. "It looks like I had better be going."

"Yes. OK," said John. "Well, thanks for coming and don't forget to tell Dad that I spoke to you." I sensed anxiety in his voice for the first time.

"Yes of course I will. Well then I'll be off . . . Look I'll see Shaun and we'll discuss it . . . If we look hard enough we might find something . . . In fact we may well do just that . . ." I paused realizing that I was rambling. I then made a decision. "Look John, I will study your case. It may be that all is not lost, not yet anyway. Would you be kind enough to tell me exactly what you remember?"

"Would you be kind enough to listen?" replied John mimicking my delivery. I had less than five minutes in which to hear the story that the *Code of Silence* had blocked for so long.

John told his story clearly and carefully but was at pains to stress that it was based mainly on what other people had told him because his own memory of the night of the 22nd/23rd April 1989 was extremely limited. He was able to recall the events leading up to the time the Druids arrived at Scarborough Mere very clearly. However, he admitted that throughout the evening he had consumed an enormous amount of alcohol consisting mainly of lager and a vicious cocktail of vodka and Coca Cola.

He had also taken a large number of pain killing tablets which had been prescribed for him only the week before after he had injured his leg and elbow in a motorcycle accident. The injuries had left him in constant pain which was aggravated by the cold weather he had encountered on the *run* from Rotherham to Scarborough.

I was later to speak to an old friend, Dr. Robert Evans of St. James's University Hospital in Leeds who prepared a report on how such a mixture would affect a person.

The report emphasized that John's state of mind would have been very confused to say the least.

The mixture of drink and drugs proved to be a potent cocktail and John was unaware of much that happened at the campsite later in the evening. He recalled being woken up by someone saying, "You had better go with them." And so he stumbled after the group who were walking away from the camp. He thought he was going downhill and remembered falling over a tent rope. As he got up he was hit in the face and wrestled with someone who fell on top of him. He tried to push the person off but only remembered being helped back to the Druids' camp and falling into his own tent. The next thing he could recall was being woken by the police later in the morning.

John's story would have been unremarkable except for the fact that the person he had wrestled with was Stephen Rowley and by the time he fell on top of John, Rowley was already dead.

Rather than telling his story to the police, John chose to follow the rules of the Druids Motorcyle Club, specifically Rule 9 which states: *No statements to be made to any police.* The only statement he made was that he knew nothing of the attack.

As a legal exercise, there was nothing wrong with John's conviction as he had clearly lied to the police when he said that he had no contact with Rowley and he was unwilling to account for the presence of Rowley's blood on his clothes. Also, when he came to trial he refused to give evidence which meant that the jury were faced with three unanswered questions. Firstly, why did he lie? Secondly, how had Rowley's blood got onto his clothing? And finally, why would he not give evidence?

No defendant is required to give evidence in a criminal trial and he is perfectly within his rights to decline to do so. Indeed juries should be warned that no inferences can be taken from a defendant's decision not to give evidence. However, in reality, the jury, in the light of other factors in the case, were likely to have taken his refusal to speak into account when finding him guity. From the evidence, the jury would have seen two options: he had either done it or he was covering up for someone else.

I put these points to John and he wholeheartedly agreed with my assumptions. I then pointed out that at no time during the trial had his defence suggested that he might have been covering up for someone else. Therefore, in the absence of any explanation from John, the jury would have been drawn irresistably to the conclusion that John was guilty of murder.

I went on to question John about how far he had got with an appeal as there had been much talk about one and indeed counsel had settled grounds on the basis that the question of provocation had not been put to the jury. I saw a problem with this as provocation implies that the accused actually committed the deed but was forced into it by the victim's unreasonable conduct. I believed that there was no possibility of an appeal on this basis as the judge had not made any mistakes during his summing up and more importantly John was saying that he had not done the deed.

It is not possible to appeal on the basis that the defendant is dissatisfied with the jury's decision. There has to be some fault found in the judge's summing up or a point of law that could be raised. As neither were present in John's case, it seemed that the only options were to persuade the Home Secretary to review the case or to find some other ground for appeal, namely fresh evidence.

I felt the first option was unlikely to succeed because John had certainly played his own part in getting convicted in the first place. The only other possibility was for someone to come forward and to reveal new evidence about the murder itself. Fresh evidence must be new evidence and evidence that was not available at the time of the trial.

The only fresh eyewitness evidence would have to come from a member of the Druids as they were the only ones present at the scene. However, they had already given statements to the police declaring that they knew nothing and therefore any statements they could make now would not be regarded as new evidence.

John knew that things didn't look good and I could only agree adding rather forlornly that it had been a much easier case to prosecute than to defend. It was apparent that John had conditioned himself to face the life sentence fully aware that he shouldn't have to but realizing that he only had himself to blame. He was very disappointed at the way his fellow Druids had treated him as he had adhered to the *bikers' code* to the letter. He had believed that his friends would stand by him but they had stopped visiting him as soon as he had been sentenced. To make matters worse, while John was on trial in Leeds, the Druids had sold his motorcycle and had spent the proceeds on drink.

I told him that if I was serving a sentence for someone else, I would not be able to stop shouting about it until I went mad. John, with a wry smile, replied with, "I don't have any option. If I dwelt on it for too long it would drive me mad."

He had taught himself to accept that he would serve his time and there was little point in getting upset about it. Perhaps this level of acceptance encapsulated a fatalism which made his cross a little easier to bear.

At this point, the prison officer returned, signalling the end of the visit. I didn't want to leave because I still had many questions to ask. I had already agreed to contact the other Druids and ask them to see me as John was sure that they would talk to me. I had serious doubts that any of them would come forward now but not wanting to insult John I agreed to try. My last question was to ask John if he had seen anyone involved in the case since he began serving his sentence. I felt that anyone who cared enough to visit might be willing to help. However, his answer, which took some getting out of him, shocked me. As he had not welcomed the visit or believed it of any importance, he had almost erased it from his memory. He told me that only a few weeks after he had been sentenced the police had visited him to ask him who had really murdered Stephen Rowley. I was so stunned by his revelation that I had to ask him to repeat what he had just said.

Why would the police visit him at all? The case was closed and their job was done. Why on earth would they wish to see him and, more importantly, why would they ask him who had really done it? I realized that something was very, very wrong. Obviousy, the police were not convinced that the right man had been put behind bars and the longer I spent with John Megson, the more I began to think that he may be innocent of murder.

We shook hands again but this time it was the *solidarity* handshake, our forearms pointing upwards and our right hands clasped in a thumbs-linked, fingers over the side position. It was a signal of a greater understanding between us and I couldn't help thinking how unusual it was to find such a man in such a place. Here was a man with too much pride and dignity to ask for anything. There had been no requests for cigarettes, postal orders or *Red Cross parcels*. Two years of imprisonment had not removed his self-respect. In the months and years to come whenever I thought we might not succeed I only had to recall that first meeting to give me the determination to carry on.

As John was led away from the inmates side of the interview room and back into the main part of the prison, I realized that although he knew he was innocent of murder he had accepted that he would serve the remainder of his life sentence for someone else; for someone who had disregarded the *code* that John held so dear.

As I waited in the queue for my *release* I went over in my mind the meeting I had just had, locking the important points into my memory. I was herded with the other visitors from one security section to another, each time the electronically operated doors opening and closing in such a way to prevent the opportunity of any inmate escaping with the visitors. As the last door closed behind me I couldn't help thinking of the young man I had left inside. However I also thought of another young man, Stephen Rowley who I would never be able to meet. His murder had resulted in John Megson's life sentence which might have been some consolation to Rowley's family and friends. If Megson was proved to be innocent, even this would be taken away from them.

What if Megson was telling the truth? What if the real killer was free? What if Shaun Megson was right and everyone else was wrong? Surely not; such things are reserved for novels and films. It just doesn't happen in real life. There are too many safeguards within the British justice system. If there was any doubt, the judge would have spotted it. Yes, of course, it was a ridiculous speculation.

I drove down the motorway and tried to concentrate on the cases that would be waiting for my attention on my return to the office. Arriving back in Rotherham, I walked into a list of telephone messages as long as my arm. Karen, Peter and John, my criminal section colleagues were discussing how to accommodate the various cases we had to represent the following morning and I picked up the phone. I had only cleared a few calls when Karen asked, "Well?"

"Well what?" I replied knowing exactly what she wanted to know.

"Has he done it? You always say you can pick out a murderer when you see one." I decided at that moment.

"That bugger hasn't done it." Karen looked across at the others and raised her eyebrows. No-one spoke as I left the room. "Now what do we do?" I asked myself.

I couldn't leave John to rot in Prison. I would have to do something, but what? how? when? and with what?

I reviewed the situation. I had no case, no right of appeal, no legal aid or funds with which to work and a work schedule which would not allow for a *freebie*. However, the odds appealed to me. I was stuck with John Megson and he with me whether either or us liked it or not.

That very weekend I started work. I had a momentous task just devouring the mountains of paperwork that had been given to me. There were statements, photographs, plans and copies of exhibits, all of which had to be considered and carefully logged. The preparation work was difficult because of the sheer volume of paperwork. Owing to my weekday commitments, I had no option but to burn the midnight oil and invade my weekends as well. I remember one Sunday afternoon in particular when most lawyers are either having a snooze, walking the dog or just propping up a bar in a pub, I was sitting at my dining table, pouring over the masses of paperwork. I began to wonder why on earth I had got involved in the case. If we were on a wild goose chase and subsequently lost, I was sure that my critics would have had me sectioned under the Mental Health Act.

I wrote to the other Druids to see if they were prepared to see me, but unfortunately, although not surprisingly, they failed to respond. Eventually I heard from Snake (Brian Frankham) and had a very short meeting with him at my office. He told me that he knew nothing of the incident as he was asleep at the time. After explaining that he could not add anything to the statement he had given to the police at Scarborough, he promptly left the office. I felt he had turned up to sound me out and find out what I knew. We were both disappointed.

I also began to put feelers out in the hope that the *jungle drums* would begin to work. On one occasion when I was in the local magistrates' court corridor drinking a cup of WRVS coffee, I was approached by a motley looking fellow wearing a leather jacket and a tee-shirt with the word *Bollocks* emblazoned upon it. Having heard that I was making enquiries into the Megson case, he asked me about it. I will never discuss cases with anyone without my clients' consent, but I was keen to hear what he had to say. "He didn't stab that lad, you know," he said positively.

"What makes you say that?" I asked curiously.

"Well," he went on, "The word on the street is that somebody else did it and your bloke got the rap'.

"How sure are you of that?" I asked.

"Quite sure old cock," he swaggered, "Your problem is going to be proving it. No bugger dare open his mouth for fear of having it filled in. Shame that, he's not a bad bloke either."

"Even more reason to prove it, then," I said invitingly.

"Rather you than me my old cock, but all the best anyway."

This was not the only time that I was approached in this way. The criminal fraternity love to *tittle tattle* and informing upon others for the sheer hell of it is an art form. What was apparent, however, was that *the drums* were all playing the same tune and more often than not, the *word on the street* is worthy, at the very least, of consideration. What did reassure me, was that no one was telling me John had done it and, while I didn't need convincing, such comments only added to my determination to succeed. The difficulty is that such information cannot be used in a court of law, but it can sometimes be a good indicator of the truth.

I have seen many cases before the courts where a great many of the facts have been withheld from the jury because of the admissibility rules. Although, at times this is extremely frustrating for both the prosecution and the defence, it is the way the system works in an attempt to be fair to all.

I kept notes of all the conversations I had and the telephone calls I made to help me with the preparation of the case. When I was spoken to in confidence, I honoured that confidence and the names and addresses were left out so that no one else would be able to see who had said what. These boxes of notes, letters and general information proved to be of great assistance later in the proceedings.

John filled in the gaps where he could and I was soon able to refer to the police statements and the facts of the case from a position of knowledge.

III

The Murder Scene

Then someone spake: "Behold! it was a crime
Of sense avenged by sense that wore with
time."
Another said: "The crime of sense became
The crime of malice and is equal blame."
And one: He had not wholly quench'd his
power;
A little grain of conscience made him sour."
At last I heard a voice upon the slope
Cry to the summit, "Is there any hope?"

Tennyson, The Vision of Sin

My initial view of the case was that the North Yorkshire Police had come up against a wall of silence and had accepted that there was little they could do. However on a more detailed study of the statements, it was obvious that they had made a very determined effort to discover the truth.

I found that evidence in the case consisted of over two thousand pages of statements from over one hundred and sixty witnesses with some of those witnesses making more than one statement. After meeting two of the officers involved, I discovered that they had carried out more work than was recorded in the statements. For example, they had visited Rotherham on a number of occasions after the Druids had been released on bail having given their first statements. The police had undertaken secret surveillance work on the Druids' clubhouse in Fitzwilliam Road, Rotherham, watching the group's movements to and from the building.

I uncovered these facts by listening to all the police interview tapes. During one interview with Nick (Nicholas Woodhead) the police tell him that he had been seen arriving at the clubhouse with his girlfriend Josephine. This was one fact that, seemingly unimportant at the time, was to become extremely important to our case.

The police had drafted in a number of officers from other areas and more than sixty of these had made statements. I listened to them all but it would be unrealistic for me to deal with each individual statement that was put before the court. A large number of them took the form of evidence which was agreed. This means that there was nothing controversial about the evidence which for the most part was background information which the defence agreed and which could be summarized before dealing with the main evidence.

It is not unusual in criminal cases for there to be a measure of agreement between the prosecution and the defence and in such cases the evidence can be read to the jury or indeed handed to the defence for them to use if they think it helpful to their case.

The police had interviewed most if not all of the people who were around the Mere on the night of 22nd/23rd April 1989. They had also questioned the landlords and customers of the public houses that the Druids had visited that day. Their aim was to establish their movements in order to build a case against them.

The Druids would certainly stand out in a crowd and were likely to be remembered. Also the public tend to have preconceived ideas about how bikers act and would therefore keep a close eye on their activities. This resulted in the police being able to formulate a very clear picture of the Druids' movements that night.

Beginning with their visit to the Victoria Wine Shop in Scarborough, the Druids stocked up with alcohol for their evening's entertainment. The assistants at the shop were able to give the police detailed information because due to the group's behaviour, they had been watched very closely. The manager gave very good descriptions of the men who visited his store and these proved to be remarkably accurate. When the police showed the staff photographs, one assistant recognized Snake (Brian Frankham) and Geordie (George Palmer). Another assistant remembered someone buying a full bottle of Smirnoff Vodka together with a plastic bottle of Coca-Cola. The till roll recorded the exact time of purchase and all the items bought, which included: a quarter bottle of Smirnoff Red Label Vodka, cans of McEwan's Bitter, Tetley Bitter, cider, lager, a concoction called Red Label Thunderbird, other assorted canned drinks and various packets of crisps and nuts. The size of the purchases suggested that the group were preparing to have a party that night. This sort of detailed information is often used by the police to unsettle suspects and to imply that they know more than they actually do resulting in the suspect telling them more than they had intended to.

One of the assistants in the shop spoke of feeling

intimidated by the Druids but admitted that this was more to do with their general appearance and the reputation of bikers than anything that they actually did. It seemed that the entire group was in good spirits and there had been no reports of any trouble that evening. Indeed when one landlord expressed some concern about their presence in his pub and asked them to leave, they did so without any hostility.

After an advanced party of Mex (John Megson) and Adie (Adrian Holmes) had found a suitable campsite, the Druids descended upon Scarborough Mere. The group arrived at about 11pm and having put up their various tents began building a camp fire.

A local security firm that specialized in the security cover of sports events had got the job of looking after the area around the Mere. As the Oliver's Mount Motorcycle Races were an annual event that attracted enthusiasts from all over the country, the security firm had employed a number of people on a temporary basis to act as extra security guards. Among these were Gary Metcalf and Geoffrey Smith. Their duties on the night of the murder were to patrol the Oliver's Mount area making sure that no unauthorized people were able to get into the competitors' enclosure. During the evening they carried out a number of patrols and when the area began to settle down for the night they intended to return to the caravan provided by their company where they would sign off duty and get some sleep.

Just after midnight, the two guards decided to patrol on foot along the perimeter road around the Mere where they had seen some camp fires. They intended to make sure that the fires were safe before the people nearby went to sleep. As there were many cars and motorcycles in the area, they were concerned that a fire could easily spread if reasonable precautions were not taken.

Within a short time they arrived at the Rowley encampment where music was being played and where they were given two cans of lager. The group of young men were enjoying themselves and all seemed well. Gary Metcalf and Geoffrey Smith walked on about fifty metres where, on the other side of the road, they saw a group of about twelve motorcyclists standing around a camp fire. The group, all dressed in "Hell's Angels' gear' was a mix of men and women. These were the Druids.

The security men spoke to them about the fire, and the Druids complained about a pick-up truck which had been racing past them and in their opinion was being driven dangerously. One of the security men remembered speaking to a man who he described as 6'6" tall, heavily built, with a long straggly beard. He was wearing a dirty white tee-shirt with some sort of logo on the front, a sleeveless denim jacket and jeans with holes in them. This description fitted Geordie (George Palmer), who they were to recognize when they saw him later in the police van. The security men said that his manner was quite pleasant and while he had obviously had a lot to drink, he was not drunk. The other members of the group were in a similar condition.

Having complained about the activity of the pick-up truck, the Druids made it plain that unless the security guards told the driver to calm down they would put him in the lake. However, the guards were not too concerned about the matter and decided not to take any action, and left the Druids to get on with their party.

The Druids had spent the evening indulging in one of their favourite pastimes, which was drinking alcohol and generally messing around. They played various games including one which involved tripping one another up. There appeared to be no hostility until one of them, Animal (Colin McCombie), took exception to a group further up the Mere who were being rather noisy. This was not Rowley's encampment but some other group who were unaware of the Druids presence at the mere.

At this point Stella, who was Boggy's (Robert Owen) *ol' lady*, recalled Animal (Colin McCombie) saying that they ought to go and *stab them up*. No one appeared to take too much notice of Animal and the party continued.

There was considerable shouting and swearing between the different groups camped round the Mere and the Rowley encampment started playing music extremely loudly which appeared to incense certain members of the Druids. By 1 am Mex (John Megson) had drunk a vast amount and he was very drunk.

The Rowley encampment consisted of Stephen Rowley, Darren Lynn, Neil Drakesmith and Kevin Richardson a group of friends who had travelled down from the North East together. There were some other Geordies in the vicinity, but they were not camped with this group, although they appeared to know each other and had spent some time together earlier that evening.

Mark Edward Hudson, from County Durham, described seeing Stephen Rowley shortly after midnight. He said that Rowley was in a happy mood but not falling down drunk. For a joke, Rowley, Drakesmith and Lynn had collapsed Hudson's tent by pulling out a couple of the tent pegs. This caused considerable amusement and as Hudson was putting his tent back up, Rowley and his friends walked back towards their own camp fire.

Hudson didn't see them again that night. However, when Rowley's group got back to their tent, there was a lot of shouting across the water to Hudson's group who shouted back. Hudson told the police that he knew Stephen Rowley reasonably well. He knew him as a lad who liked a good laugh and a drink, but claimed that when in drink Rowley was neither violent, arrogant nor aggressive.

Stephen Rowley had decided to go to Scarborough for the motor cycle racing with his friends Neil Drakesmith, Darren Lynn and Kevin Richardson. On Saturday 22nd April, 1989, the group set off from their homes in Seaham in County Durham. They travelled in Neil Drakesmith's Volkswagen Golf, taking with them a change of clothes, tent and other items for the journey. Like the Druids, they too had stopped at public houses before arriving at the Mere. They also went to an off licence where Darren Lynn remembered that they bought twelve cans of Fosters Lager and twenty-four cans of Stones Bitter. They clearly had the intention of consuming a considerable amount of alcohol.

They arrived in Scarborough at about 8 pm and pitched their tent near the Mere. They decided that Rowley and Lynn would sleep in the tent and Drakesmith and Richardson in the car. They lit a fire and later on in the evening, went to a local fish and chip shop for some supper, which they ate outside the shop. They called at a public house on the way back to the Mere staying there from 9 pm until 11 pm drinking about three pints each. The group returned to the camp fire and put the radio on. Darren Lynn described the group as having a good time *larking about a bit* around the fire.

They had only been back at the tent for a short time,

when some people they knew came over to the fire. After a few minutes they left and Lynn said he was tired. He was unclear as to the time but remembered that they had all decided to turn in for the night at about 2 am. He admitted that they were all in a boisterous mood because of the amount they had drunk.

Drakesmith and Richardson got into the car and tried to go to sleep. Drakesmith was in the front and Richardson in the rear. Richardson recalled hearing Rowley and another lad, Gary Mars, laughing and joking between themselves. He remembered that their voices were very loud. They were so noisy that Darren Lynn was woken up. and he tried to get into the car with Drakesmith and Richardson, but he was refused entry so he returned to the tent. Drakesmith remembered telling Rowley to be quiet many times but he just laughed and said that he didn't want to go to sleep. Eventually, Drakesmith began to drift into sleep, but at some point his attention was drawn to the sound of voices. At first he thought that it was Rowley and Lynn, but he couldn't see outside the car because the windows had become misted over.

He then realized that there were more people than Lynn and Rowley at the tent, so he opened the car door to see what was happening. At this stage, Richardson had woken and opened the rear door when he heard Darren Lynn scream loudly. They saw a group of people near the tent, some of whom were carrying sticks or poles. Drakesmith asked what was going on, and was told to get back in the car. He believed he was told to, "Get back in the car or you will be next. You should have told them to keep quiet." One of the group put a stick towards Richardson's face. From their positions at the car, both Drakesmith and Richardson saw Rowley lying on the ground in front of the tent with Lynn standing up nearby complaining about a pain in his back.

Intimidated by the group's threat, Drakesmith and Richardson closed the car doors and watched as the group left the area but could not see where they had gone. When they were satisfied the group had left, Drakesmith and Richardson got out of the vehicle and went to Rowley. He was lying on his back and his body was covered in blood. His breathing was abnormal and Drakesmith heard the sound of choking.

Lynn had seen a little more of the incident, from inside the tent as the front of the tent was unzipped. He had heard shouting and swearing outside and so he crawled out headfirst. He felt someone grab the back of his hair and he was dragged out of the tent. He couldn't see who had grabbed him, but he felt blows immediately to his face, back and stomach.

He recounted, "I seemed to be getting hit all over the body. I believed that there was more than one person attacking me as the blows seemed to be all at once. I curled up in a ball and tried to protect myself from the attack'. He heard men swearing. "There seemed to be a lot of noise, but I didn't know what words were used. I did hear Stephen Rowley shout *Get off*."

The next thing he knew was getting to his feet and seeing Richardson standing beside his car and then walking over to help him. He saw Rowley lying on a small bank of ground approximately five metres from the tent. He could see blood everywhere, and Rowley was not moving. He remembered the ambulance arriving.

Richardson's statement is a little more detailed. He referred to opening the door of the car and seeing a group of men. Three of them were standing beside the car, directly in front of him. One prodded him in the face with his finger and said "I'm sick of all this noise. Are you with them in the tent?" Richardson's reply was that he had just woken up and had been in the car. He was told to get back in the car and before doing so he saw Darren Lynn getting off the ground and shouting for help. He got back into the car and watched the men walk off up the dirt road towards the dirt track.

Once the men had gone, he got out of the car and went to Darren Lynn and it was then that he saw Rowley laid on the ground. The scene was one of chaos and panic before the arrival of the police and the ambulance.

Richardson remembered that one of the men had a stick. He described him as having a big beer belly, wearing a black leather bike jacket and having a beard. This description fitted Geordie (George Palmer) better than anyone else. When the police arrived, they made a close inspection of the scene, took photographs and recovered a number of items.

There were no other witnesses for the prosecution who actually saw what took place.

Some other Geordies including Sharon Ross and Gary Foster arrived on the scene shortly afterwards and explained in graphic detail what they found, but they hadn't seen the incident or indeed the assailants of the two victims.

One of the first on the scene was PC Richard O'Neal and according to his statement he remembered being called to the scene at 2.35 am on Sunday 23rd April, 1989. He was met by Darren Lynn who was bleeding and appeared to be suffering some pain. He was joined by P.C. Green who attended to Darren Lynn. P.C. O'Neal was taken to see Stephen Rowley by Gary Foster and Sharon Ross. He remembered seeing a green tent which was half collapsed, a small fire smouldering and two empty sleeping bags. He then saw Rowley who was laid on his back on the ground with his arms out stretched. The officer felt for a pulse but could not find one. Rowley was cold; his eyes were open and his pupils were dilated. Inspector O'Brien and P.C. Green joined P.C. O'Neal and they all attempted to give artificial respiration to Rowley. The three officers took it in turn to give cardiac massage and artificial respiration until the ambulance arrived. Rowley's shirt had been ripped open and it was saturated in blood at the front. The officer noted that he had a wound to the left hand side of his torso near to the left nipple. This was the wound which caused his death.

The Police were able to obtain some descriptions of the assailants. Darren Lynn was unable to help, saying that he did not know who attacked him and he could not say how many there were or even describe their clothing. Neil Drakesmith described a group of people wearing *Hell's Angels* clothing, namely leather or denim trousers and jackets.

He said that they all had long hair and a couple of them had beards. He was most specific, however, about one of the Druids, who he described as having something wrong with his top teeth, namely one tooth missing or discoloured in some way. This man did not have a beard but had shoulder length, slightly wavy mid brown coloured hair and was wearing a black woollen hat. This description fitted Snake (Brian Frankham). Drakesmith described the assailants' Yorkshire accents and said that he thought they were all powerfully built.

Richardson on the other hand gave a slightly different

description. He mentioned one man who was white, approximately thirty years of age, between 5' 11" and 6' tall. He described him as stockily built with dark brown coloured hair which was shoulder length. He was wearing dirty blue denim jeans with a black leather bike jacket with full length sleeves and a denim jacket over that which had no sleeves and which was open at the front. He felt that he would have been able to recognize the man again.

He couldn't give detailed descriptions of the others, except to say that they were all about thirty years of age and wore biker type clothing. He referred to the fact that two had beards and at least one had a moustache.

Two or three of these men were wearing dark coloured baseball hats and one of them appeared to be carrying a three feet long piece of wood. He was unable to describe the man who had poked him in the face.

All the participants had a considerable amount to drink that night and indeed one or two of the other witnesses present referred to Rowley shouting and swearing. The witnesses agreed that although there had certainly been some shouting between the camps there was nothing to support the suggestion that this had provoked the attack.

The ambulance men appeared on the scene and made every effort to revive Stephen Rowley. Geoffrey Leslie White was a leading ambulance man at the time and together with his colleague Lewis Tomlinson had answered an emergency call at 2.38 am at the Scarborough Ambulance Station. The ambulance men were soon on the scene and when they arrived at the Mere they were flagged down by a number of people. They first saw Darren Lynn who was able to get into the back of the ambulance with a little assistance. He was fully conscious and the ambulance men noticed that his hands and trousers were covered in blood. The ambulance men removed his tee-shirt which was blood stained and appeared to have three small tears in it.

They found three chest wounds which they dressed. Lynn told Mr White, that he thought he had been stabbed by a group of six men.

By that time the other ambulance man, Mr Tomlinson, was attempting to resuscitate Rowley. A valiant effort was made both by the police and the ambulance men to treat Rowley.

Mr White noticed that there were no obvious signs of life and he believed Rowley had suffered some form of wound to his chest area as there was a large amount of blood around his chest and face. The condition was clearly very serious indeed and a decision was taken to move Rowley to hospital and not to wait for assistance. He was placed in the ambulance where continued attempts at resuscitation took place.

The ambulance men were clearly so intent on their task that they did not notice who was in the locality. However P.C. O'Neal in a later statement recalled passing along the unmade road section towards the murder scene. He said that on a nearside verge close to the road, he saw a group of about six scruffy looking men clustered around the embers of a small fire. As he passed by, he saw that one or two were standing and that several others were in the process of rising to their feet. They seemed intent on watching his vehicle.

The number was important because it was said that there were six or seven men involved in the actual attack. It is clear that John Megson had actually gone and fallen into his tent and had lapsed into unconsciousness after the incident. This would account for why there were six at the scene the policeman described.

The ambulance left the scene at 2.55 am and arrived at the Hospital at 3 am. Doctor Marianne Feinauer was employed as a house officer in general medicine at Scarborough Hospital at that time. She was a member of the cardiac arrest team and was on call for emergency procedures. She recalled that at 3 am on 23rd April, she was on duty at the Hospital when she received a bleeped message. She was told that an ambulance was on route to the hospital with a patient needing the full cardiac arrest team. She went to the accident unit and within a few minutes the ambulance crew brought their patient in. A Doctor Hacki, the accident and emergency house doctor and her staff were also present. The anaesthetist, Doctor Ghurye and a further medical registrar Doctor Butte also arrived within a minute or two.

On Doctor Feinauer's arrival, the ambulance crew were still performing external heart massage and this was taken over by one of the nursing staff. Doctor Ghurye inserted a tube into Stephen Rowley's lungs and began ventilation.

Every attention was given to him, but unfortunately it was discovered that Rowley's veins had collapsed.

The switchboard managed to contact the haematologist and he was told of the circumstances and asked to attend in order to cross match the blood. A further medical practitioner Mr Ayres had arrived at this time and started to perform a left thoracotomy. He then began internal heart massage. The surgical registrar arrived and assisted Mr Ayres.

During this time, at least eight bottles of haemacell were used. A blood transfusion was soon set up, but by that time it was about 3.20 am and Mr Ayres had decided that it would have been no use to give the blood to the patient.

Despite the very considerable efforts of the police, ambulance men and hospital staff, the attempts to resuscitate Stephen Rowley were unsuccessful and at 3.50 am life was pronounced extinct.

Doctor Lloyd Denmark, the pathologist who carried out a post-mortem on the body of Stephen Rowley, found that death was as a result of shock and haemorrhage due to a stab wound to the chest which penetrated the heart.

He also found that there were a number of injuries to Stephen Rowley's face and he catalogued seven separate facial injuries and various other injuries to his hand and arm. Doctor Denmark felt that death would have occurred very rapidly indeed and certainly within a matter of minutes. There were knife wounds on the body and he concluded that they could have been inflicted by a small knife, with one edge sharpened and the other partially sharpened near the tip.

The exact depth of the fatal wound was difficult to measure, but it could have been as little as 4.5 cm when allowance was made for compression of clothing and soft tissue.

Doctor Denmark found no significant defence injuries and concluded that the injuries to the face, were, with the exception of a horizontal cut across the mid point of his nose, due to an assault with blunt instruments such as fists or boots. He found one mark to the forehead which appeared to be from the sole of a boot. It was clear that Stephen Rowley had been badly beaten.

Darren Lynn had three superficial stab wounds almost in a vertical line near the centre of his back. Each one was approximately one and a half centimetres across. At the hospital he was found to be conscious and in no immediate danger. X-rays were taken which confirmed that the wounds had not penetrated the chest wall. In the doctor's opinion the wounds were no more than one centimetre deep and so they were dressed by nursing staff and, having been given an anti-tetanus injection, Lynn was moved onto a ward. One of the doctors believed that Lynn had drunk a large amount of alcohol although no tests were carried out. After a short time under observation on the ward Lynn was discharged from hospital the same day.

Back at the Mere, police reinforcements had been drafted in to ensure that no one, matching descriptions already given, left the area. At 6.30 am on Sunday 23rd April 1989 the police asked about forty people who were at the Mere to "help them with their enquiries'. The police had to wake John Megson before they could ask his help.

A plain clothes police officer was placed *undercover* in the snooker room to note any conversation that might help to clarify what had happened at the Mere. There is no record of any success with this ploy but John Megson remembered that the *undercover* officer stood out "like a sore thumb' because his clothes were clean and his trainers were brand new. The Druids had been kept under closer observation than most others in the room because they were scruffier than the rest and certain members fitted descriptions that the police were now gathering. However the Druids behaviour gave no clues as to their involvement. Indeed some of them were sleeping and those who were awake were generally silent.

The police then set about taking statements from everyone in the room. Each of the Druids were systematically interviewed. CRO (Criminal Records Office) forms, which note the clothing and physical state of the interviewees were completed and Polaroid photographs were taken.

John Megson identified himself as Derek Megson, giving his brother's name, date of birth and address. The reason for this was nothing more sinister than the fact that he had no insurance for his motorcycle and also a number of outstanding fines for motoring offences which he had not yet paid. By giving his brother's name, he had no intention of avoiding anything more than another motoring offence. If he believed he was to be accused of murder, the last thought on his mind would be his lack of proper motoring insurance.

John made a statement in which he said that he was drunk at the time of the murder and knew nothing about any events leading to the attack or surrounding the incident. P.C. Taylor noted that John Megson had sustained a recent injury to his upper lip which showed as an area of redness with a certain amount of swelling. He also had a small wound on the inside of one lip. There were also small scratch marks, which appeared to be recent, on the back of both his hands. At that time I don't believe the police had formed any opinion as to how the injury had occurred. All the Druids stuck to the same story, stating that they were either drunk or asleep at the time of the incident and that they took no part in it.

With more than forty people herded into the police station, the police had a very difficult job to do. Although it is easy to criticize with the benefit of hindsight, I believe it was at this time that they made their biggest mistake. They decided to take items of clothing from selected individuals for possible forensic testing. From the whole group present at Scarborough that night, clothing was only taken from John Megson. It would have certainly been extremely difficult to take clothing from everyone but the police's attention had already focused on the Druids and this should have made them prime targets for testing. Had other members of the Druids' clothing been taken there would have been a possiblity of blood staining being found which could have provided the police with the evidence needed to bring charges against them.

The police attempted to rectify this error when certain members were re-arrested in May 1989 but by this time there was nothing to prove that the clothing taken was the same clothing that had been worn on the night or that it hadn't been tampered with. If only the police had taken some of the clothing of the other members of the Druids on Sunday 23rd April 1989 the real killer may well have been brought to justice at that time.

When all the Druids had been interviewed, they were released in order that the police could complete their enquiries. They had not been arrested and there was no legal justification for detaining any of them at that time.

The officer in charge of the enquiry was Detective Superintendent George Herbert Chadwick, a very experienced policeman who supervised the collection of all the evidence. From the wealth of material that I was given access to, it was obvious that he had gone to great lengths to obtain the evidence to bring some convictions for this brutal killing.

The police set about collating all the information they had gathered. A large number of officers had visited the Mere taking many photographs and a video film. They went through the area *with a fine-tooth comb* even collecting a glove and a Biro that a policeman had lost on the night of the murder. A number of items had been taken from the murder scene including a scarf, a glove, drinks cans and even cigarette ends. P.C. Jones had found one sinister item near the Druids encampment. This item appeared to be a knuckle duster with a knife blade incorporated in the handle. This was found partially buried with only four centimetres showing above the ground. Many items were sent to the Forensic Science Laboratory at Harrogate for testing but no weapon which could be directly linked to the murder was ever found.

Meanwhile, blood samples that had been taken from Stephen Rowley and Darren Lynn were analysed and it was discovered that Rowley's blood group was rare, with only one person in thirty eight thousand sharing his group.

Soon afterwards, the police received the report from the Forensic Science Laboratory. It had been completed by Sara Catriona Gray, a Home Office scientist who had inspected John Megson's clothing. The following items had been studied:

1. Boots
2. Socks
3 Leather Motorcycle Jacket
4 Denim Jacket
5 Outer jacket
6 Inner Pullover

7 Inner Shirt
8 Belt and Pouch
9 Denim Jeans
10 Leather Trousers
11 Underpants

It was discovered that John's leather jacket had blood-staining on the inside and outside of the left cuff, on the left sleeve and on both lapels. His pullover had blood staining on each cuff and several spots of blood on the upper front. The blood stains were found to be of the same blood group as Stephen Rowley. While the scientist had not carried out a full D.N.A. test which would have been preferred, it was fairly certain that there had been contact between John Megson and Stephen Rowely. The scarf found at the scene was also found to have blood stains which matched Rowley's blood group.

The police clearly had the breakthrough they required and so, armed with the forensic evidence, they set out to Rotherham to bring the Druids back to Scarborough for further questioning. John Megson was the first to be arrested on Tuesday 9th May 1989. Other arrests followed with the suspects being taken to various police stations in order to reduce the possibility of any of them passing on information received during their questioning.

IV

The Conspiracy

> "For now I see the true old times are dead,
> When every morning brought a noble chance,
> And every chance brought out a noble knight."
>
> *Tennyson*, Morte D'Arthur

When the Druids were released from Scarborough Police Station, on Sunday 23rd April 1989 they gathered their belongings and returned to Rotherham.

On their arrival, they went straight to the club house and began a discussion about the weekend's events. The president, Bandy [Ray Millward] was extremely annoyed because some of the members had allowed the police to take their *Colours* for forensic tests. *The colours* are the most important part of the bikers' culture, almost like the flag standard of a regiment, when it comes to comparing the pride and passions of membership.

The colours or *patches* are the club badge which are stitched onto the back of a denim jacket. When Snake (Brian Frankham) was arrested at the camp site a police officer seized his *Colours* and threw them onto the seat of a police car. Frankham was seen to pick them up, fold them carefully, indeed, almost reverently before putting them back on the seat. The police officer was keen to mention this in his statement.

At the club house, each member related the events as they remembered them. John Megson remained silent due to the fact that he remembered so little of what had happened.

It was clear that Animal (Colin McCombie) was heavily involved and was known to carry a knife. Yettie (Simon Negrotti), on the other hand claimed to have performed one of the acts of violence, but no one took him seriously as he had a reputation for exaggerating. A further meeting was arranged for the following day which was to be attended by all the members and their respective *ol' ladies*. This was an unusual demand because meetings at the club house were normally attended by the Druids only. Women were not allowed to be involved and therefore had no voice. But these were unusual times and unknown to the Druids, outside the clubhouse were members of the North Yorkshire Police.

The police had secreted themselves in unmarked cars near the Druids' club house. They were watching the comings and goings of the various members and their partners and were later able to question the Druids about this during the second series of interviews.

I listened to these taped interviews with interest as the police quite correctly tried to trip the Druids up when they tried to deny attending the meetings which were held in order to reach an agreement on the story they would tell the police. It was apparent from their reactions on tape that the Druids were totally unaware of the police presence.

At the second meeting, Snake (Brian Frankham) had

prepared a statement setting out the events as far as he was concerned. This document was later seized by the police when Snake was arrested. It was clear that the main concern of the Druids centred on Animal (Colin McCombie).

John Megson's behaviour was not discussed at the clubhouse, as he had done little and certainly was not responsible for the stabbing of Rowley and Lynn. However, the Druids agreed that all of the stories given to the police must match.

It was agreed that no one would admit anything and certainly there would be no mention of any other member. If the wrong person was charged and was one of the Druids, the guilty parties would have to come forward and clear their fellow members. Only John Megson was to observe the agreement and only John Megson was to begin a life sentence.

I have found in criminal cases that generally speaking *there is no honour among thieves*. My former senior partner George Tierney used to say that you could not expect loyalty from people who are prepared to indulge in criminal behaviour in the first place. In my view, he was right and in this case promises of *all for one and one for all* gave way to *every man for himself*. The one exception being John Megson.

The Druids believed that they would be questioned again by the police and so they were keen to ensure that everyone knew exactly what they had to do. There was no flexibility in this arrangement. When all matters were agreed, the Druids went about their day to day business and waited.

V

The Arrests

"Thou hast betray'd thy nature and thy name,
Not rendering true answer, as beseem'd
Thy fealty, nor like a noble knight;
For surer sign had follow'd either hand,
Or voice, or else a motion of the mere.
This is a shameful thing for men to lie."

Tennyson, Morte D'Arthur

John Megson was arrested at 6.25 am on Tuesday 9th May, 1989 by Detective Sergeant Bell. There were five other officers present.

He identified himself and then D.S. Bell told him that he was being arrested on suspicion of the murder of Stephen Rowley. John's recorded reply was:

"You what? Murder? Me? You've got to be joking!"

He was taken to Scarborough Police Station where he arrived at 8.20 am.

He was processed and placed in a police cell.

He stayed there until 12.30 pm when his first interview took place and over the next few days he was interviewed eight times.

At 6.40 pm on Wednesday 10th May, 1989, he was charged with murder. His only reply was:-

"Not Guilty to it."

Over the next three days the other Druids were arrested and taken to various police stations in the Scarborough area.

As with many similar cases the police relied upon the waiting game. All a defendant can do is to sit, wait and ponder as to what his fellow defendants may have said. During this time of uncertainty, they can make mistakes. Their curiosity gets the better of them and often they will say something that conflicts with what has been said by another defendant. This is when the police are able to tie a suspect up so that they either show themselves to be liars or the police do it for them.

Interviewing a suspect is a skilled job. Techniques can be taught but some officers are naturals and with experience and training they become very proficient inquisitors.

Times have changed, however, and in the past five years I have noticed a substantial change in the way that the police conduct interviews. The tape recording procedure removes a great deal of dispute as a copy of the tape is always available to the defence and the court and is obviously a true record of what has been said, not only by the defendant but also by the police.

Before tape recording, interviews were conducted by way of contemporaneous notes or the police completing a record of the interviews from memory. The latter course was always unsuitable in my view as it was open to abuse and error. So many of the cases that were subject to appeal featured allegations of admissions being made to the police either under duress or being falsely recorded. The tape recording procedure removes these possibilities to a considerable extent.

The interviews in the Megson case made for fascinating listening.

The officer who stands out in my memory most of all was George Lickes. He was an experienced officer who finished his service shortly after the John Megson case. It is a loss to the police service as he had the most amazing interview technique I had ever heard.

I was later informed by one of the officers in the case that if George Lickes couldn't get a *cough*, police slang for an admission of guilt, no one could.

Lickes did not interview all the Druids but he did interview Animal (Colin McCombie).

McCombie was compliant during the initial interview but eventually George Lickes was starting to get under his skin and McCombie was wise enough to know it. When he was told that John Megson had been charged with murder, he caught his breath. He then refused to answer any further questions. The police noted that he was shaking with fear at the beginning of one interview and try as he might, McCombie could not pull himself together. Fearing that the police had realized that they had touched a nerve, he refused to say anything further. That was until George Lickes got under his skin again.

George Lickes referred to Rowley's parents and the grieving that they had sustained. He referred to McCombie's own child, and asked him how he would have felt if someone had done anything to her. He suggested that McCombie should speak out and tell the truth. He accused McCombie of being involved in the murder with such intensity that I believe he thought him responsible. This tape and this accusation was never reported in the evidence served upon the defence. I suppose that it could be argued that it was not of any evidential value but it certainly made me think.

The rest of the tapes showed how well the Druids had rehearsed. The easiest way of avoiding being tripped up is to say nothing or to say you cannot remember. It conceals a multitude of sins.

One can only speculate as to what would have happened if the clothing of Animal (Colin McCombie) had been seized at the Mere. The Police may have been in a position to break his silence as they did with John Megson, but in this case there may not have been an explanation. Rowley could not have fallen onto them all. The Druids' Code of Silence was observed to a point. The point was to enable the group to save themselves and to leave John Megson to his fate.

When I acquired the tapes of John's interviews, I was intrigued by one of them. In it, the police suggested to him that he was covering up for someone else. If he was, the police advised, he should say so and save himself. He did not heed the warning.

I don't believe that the others would have kept silent if they had been charged with murder, but I suppose we will never know now. Only John Megson was charged with murder and Adie (Adrian Holmes) was charged with Violent Disorder.

George Lickes made the point to Animal (Colin McCombie) that the Druids were a pathetic bunch with no morals, loyalties or scruples. McCombie chose not to reply.

VI

The Defence Case

He that wrongs his friend
Wrongs himself more, and ever bears about
A silent court of justice in his breast,
Himself the judge and jury and himself
The prisoner at the bar, ever condemned.

Tennyson

John Megson was brought before the Leeds Crown Court for trial on the 13th July, 1990.

He was represented by two barristers from Sheffield, Roger Keen and Andrew Hatton.

Throughout the trial, John was expecting his so-called friends to appear in force. They of course had been promising the earth, but they never arrived. John's friend Stephen Thomas a fellow member of the Druids and Elaine Jubb, John's girlfriend at the time attended the trial to give John whatever support they could. The remaining members of the Druids were conspicuous by their absence.

John's defence had always been that he was not responsible for the stabbing of Stephen Rowley and indeed was not at the murder scene.

In the light of the forensic evidence, John had little or no chance of sustaining a reasoned and coherent defence. To give a truthful account would compromise him with his friends and with the *Code of Silence*. John had given his conditional agreement that he would remain silent.

The only issue that seemed to be taken was a fairly obscure point on the question of the blood samples.

The prosecution were not able to say categorically that the blood on John Megson's clothing belonged to Stephen Rowley, but they were able to point to its rarity. The prosecution therefore, contended that Rowley's blood was on John Megson's clothes.

John's own blood group had been determined, as had the groups of the other Druids and none of their blood groups matched that of Stephen Rowley.

The defence made the point that no one could be certain that it was Rowley's blood but it was a weak defence point and in my view it was quite reasonable for the jury to disregard it.

After about two days of the trial and following the acquittal of Holmes, it became obvious to John that the Druids were not going to support him. It is some measure of the hold that the Druids had over him, that it took him so long to realize this. It was then, in desperation and most certainly confusion, that he spoke out.

John told me that he told his legal representatives that he knew who had committed the stabbing. However, he was unable to give that evidence because it meant breaching the Code and implicating one of his colleagues. He refused to give the name, but it is obvious that he was in a state of panic at the time.

There can be no doubt that he placed his legal representatives in an intolerable position. They could not call

John to give evidence to say anything other than the truth. They knew that John Megson knew who the killer was and for them to allow him to give evidence contrary to the truth would have drawn them into a conspiracy. The ethics of the situation do not allow lawyers to do that and I am sure they attempted to persuade John to go into the witness box and speak the truth.

John refused to give evidence himself and no one else had been prepared to give evidence for him. There would be no explanation of the forensic evidence, and the fact that the jury didn't hear what John had to say, must have helped the jury to decide that he was guilty.

The prosecution team was led by Martin Bethel Q.C., a very able Queen's Counsel from Leeds. His junior was Andrew Robertson, also an experienced Counsel.

It is appropriate at this point to explain the differences between a Q.C. and a Junior Counsel and why certain cases require two barristers rather than one. All barristers are called Junior Counsel. When Junior Counsel acquire seniority they can apply to take silk. If successful, the Junior Counsel becomes Leading Counsel or Queen's Counsel as the position is better known. Not all Junior Counsel become Q.C.s. The position is reserved for barristers of seniority with standing in the legal profession.

Tradition requires that if a Q. C. is involved in a case, he has to have a Junior Counsel with him and certainly until recently it has been most unusual to have a Q. C. appear on his own.

The general theory is that the Junior Counsel does all the spade work and refers the important points to the Q.C. who normally takes the position of being the *front man* conducting the case before the court. This simplified description is probably sufficient to understand the roles of Q.C. and Junior Counsel in the John Megson case.

The prosecution put their case on the basis that John was the actual stabber. This was interesting because in the preparation for the appeal when we were to show by our own forensic evidence that John was not the stabber, the prosecution moved their ground somewhat. They were to say that as John was a member of the gang and as he was present when Rowley was stabbed, he was still guilty of murder by reason of *Joint Enterprise*.

Someone who is a party to a joint enterprise, the carrying out of which results in a death, may be criminally liable for that death on the basis that he is guilty of murder or that he is guilty of manslaughter.

It is fundamental to a conviction for either offence that the accused must have been party to the act which caused the death. The application of the Law concerning joint enterprise in cases of murder raises two problems:

1. Whether in the circumstances the accused was party to the act which caused death.
2. If he was, whether his state of mind was such as to make him guilty of murder or of manslaughter.

Where two or more persons embark on a joint enterprise, each is liable for the acts done in pursuance of that joint enterprise. That includes liability for unusual consequences if they arise from the execution of the agreed joint enterprise. However, if a participant in the venture goes beyond what has been tacitly agreed as part of the common enterprise, the other participant or participants is/are not liable for the consequences of that unauthorised act. There follows a number of examples which should help clarify the term *Joint Enterprise.*

In the case of Regina -v- Reid [1976] Cr.App.A. 109 C.A. the court in a reserved judgement applied the distinction drawn in R. -v- Anderson and Morris [1966] 50 Cr.App.A. 216 CCA. between a "mere unforeseen consequence of an unlawful act," [for which the accused would be liable] and "an overwhelmingly supervening event which is of such a character that it will relegate into history, matters that would otherwise be looked on as causative factors." The courts said:

"When two or more men go out together in joint possession of offensive weapons such as revolvers and knives and the circumstances are such as to justify an inference that the very least they intend to do with them is to cause fear in another, there is, in our judgement, always a likelihood that, in the excitement and tensions of the occasion, one of them will use his weapon in some way which will cause death or serious injury. If such injury was not intended by the others they must be acquitted of murder, but having started out on an enterprise which envisaged some degree of violence, albeit nothing more than causing fright, they will be guilty of manslaughter."

An example of what can happen is found in the case of R -v- Salmon [1880] 6.Q.B.D. 79. which held that if three men amused themselves by shooting a rifle at a target without taking proper precautions to prevent injury to others and one of the shots killed a man. All three are guilty of manslaughter, although there is no proof which of the three fired the fatal shot.

> Another helpful example is found in the case of R -v- White and Richardson [1806 R and R 99] which held that the act must be the result of the confederacy, for, if several are out for the purpose of commiting an offence and, upon alarm, and pursuit run different ways, and one of them kills a pursuer to avoid being taken, the others are not to be considered as aiders and abettors in that offence.

Mr Bethel had an easy case to deal with, and it wasn't long after the Judge's summing that the Jury returned to find John guilty.

John's girlfriend Elaine Jubb later described how devastated he was with the result. This was probably true, but he certainly could not have been surprised, because if there was ever a case where a man was going to be found guilty, this was it.

John later described to me how the defence team, *did their best with what they had got*. He accepted that he was of little assistance to them because of his reluctance to give evidence. I have since wondered what the jury must have thought on seeing John acquitted of the murder at Teesside in May 1994. They would be entitled to say that John brought the conviction upon himself and that if they had known the full extent of the defence, they would not have convicted him. If it eases their conscience, then so be it. I can well understand why he was convicted and can make no complaint to them, or indeed to those who represented him. It just goes to show how things can go terribly wrong when a defendant will not listen to his advisors. I have found on numerous occasions defendants who knew best and who would not take the advice of members of the legal profession with many years experience of the legal system. This was not the case with John, because there were outside influences operating upon him and from what I gather from Mr Hatton the Junior Counsel on the defence team, John was a perfectly pleasant and reasonable man, apart from his refusal to give evidence.

The Judge pronounced a life sentence which was mandatory and recommended that he serve not less than fifteen years.

John was taken from the court back to Armley Jail where he languished for some time before being transferred to the *lifer's wing* at Wakefield Prison.

Most defendants would have opened up and *grassed* on their mates. Most defendants would complain and gripe and indeed most do even when they have been convicted justly. However, there is a very old maxim used in prison which goes as follows:

If you can't do the time, don't do the crime.

All my working life I have had to put up with the whingers and the whiners and there are very few who heed that old maxim. In John Megson there was a man who was innocent of what the prosecution had alleged. He knew that the guilty party was at liberty and had got away with the crime. Nevertheless, he did not send any begging letters, he did not grumble or snivel and inexplicably he blamed no one but himself.

Shaun, his father, had not been at the trial because, despite his attempts to get information, he had not been notified of the actual hearing date. He had done his best to persuade John to tell the truth and I believe that he was not told about the hearing because John saw his father's presence as a threat to the Code.

John was visited in Armley Jail by Snake (Brian

Frankham), Geordie (George Palmer) and Yettie (Simon Negrotti), who explained their absence from the trial by claiming that they had been advised not to appear by John's legal representatives. They told John that they were taking steps to pursue an appeal on his behalf. I found it very difficult to accept that John still believed in them by this time. However, over the next few months as I considered the evidence and particularly when I listened to all the tapes of interviews with the Druids, I understood how he had formed that belief. But with the exception of Yettie (Simon Negrotti), not one of the Druids was helpful to the police as far as John was concerned. They obviously didn't want to commit themselves in any way by implicating other members of the group.

Of course, they were in a different position as none of them were charged with murder, but John believed that they would have acted in the same way had the roles been reversed. I very much doubted it.

Snake (Brian Frankham) and the others told John that they were seeing a Q.C. privately and had paid him £140.00 for advice on how to proceed with the case. This was clearly a lie because a Q.C. would not give advice to others concerning a defendant and most certainly no Q.C. would give an interview for £140.00.

Nevertheless, John believed them.

I believe that they were simply trying to appease John until his time for appeal was over, whereupon the case would be closed and they would be in the clear.

The Druids' visits soon stopped and only John's family and friends continued to see him.

After the conviction, advice was given by his barristers

on the question of appeal and the view was taken that an appeal might lie on the grounds that the judge had not referred the jury to the question of provocation. Grounds for appeal were settled and lodged at the Court of Appeal on that basis.

VII

Time In Prison

> Liberty is one of the most precious gifts that Heaven has bestowed on man and captivity is the greatest evil that can befall him.
>
> *Cervantes*

John was re-arrested on 10th May, 1989, and he remained in a custodial setting until his release on 20th May 1994. At first he was taken to Armley Jail, Leeds which is a grey forbidding place built in the style of a castle. It is approximately one hundred years old and many of the cells remain as they were originally built. There are no toilets or washbasins in the cells, and the only toilet facilities consist of a bucket placed in a corner.

The buckets are only emptied at *slopping-out time* each morning. This means that whatever has accrued during the day is kept in the buckets until the following morning. Many people would say that it is a prison and it is not meant to be pleasant. However the cells built for one person one hundred years ago now often contain two or three people and if only one has an odour problem the atmosphere can become extremely offensive.

There are horror stories about remand prisons, particularly from the point of view of those who are physically weak and unable to defend themselves. They are often the targets for bullying and intimidation. It is rather like the law of the jungle where only the strong survive and the weak fall by the wayside.

Some defendants report that they are robbed when they are placed inside. They have clothing taken and whatever belongings they have can be stolen. There are some defendants who have had their meals taken from them. The only answer to their complaints would be to tell them to go to the authorities, but few do as they fear reprisals. However, if you are not easily intimidated, life can be considerably easier and John was not the sort of man who would succumb readily to intimidation from any source.

Having gone through the booking in procedure John was shown to his cell, but he found that it was occupied by a pervert who was in the process of inserting a small plastic bottle into his anus. Many prisoners would have simply gone into the cell and hoped for the best, but John made it quite plain that unless he was moved there would be trouble. He was moved.

One of the difficulties in Armley is that the system quickly categorizes each inmate. John was immediately classified as a *trouble-maker* a tag which he could have carried throughout his prison term and which was very difficult for him to get rid of.

John had few possessions and indeed those he had, needed to be carried round with him for fear of theft. As a man who could not be intimidated, John did not experience any difficulties with other prisoners. However, he did have difficulties with certain *screws*, the colloquial term for prison officers.

John was often in trouble with the authorities at Armley but maintained throughout that this was because he was only protecting his rights as he saw them. He was often *Down the block* which is the punishment wing of the prison. John was not a trouble-maker, but if he saw himself being singled out for bad treatment or if any of his rights were denied him, he would be the first to complain. The regime also allowed any sign of weakness to be taken advantage of. With all the difficulties John had to cope with, the worst by far must have been the knowledge that he was inside for something that he hadn't done.

However, throughout his time at Armley he supported himself with the belief that his so-called friends would come forward and prove his innocence, which would result in his release. He would then have been true to the *Code of Silence* and he could not have been seen by any of his fellow Druids to have let anyone down.

John spent approximately a year in Armley leading up to his trial and following his conviction. He was then sent to Wakefield Prison where he was to remain until the appeal in February 1994. Life was better at Wakefield. He was allowed his guitar and he used the time to take courses in Engineering which he found kept his mind as active as possible and provided a foil for depression and boredom. His incarceration was broken only by visits from his family and friends. The regime in Wakefield was strict because it houses a number of *lifers* and long term prisoners but the important thing about Wakefield was that everybody knew where they stood and what the rules and regulations were. Not only did the prisoners work within that framework but so did the prison officers. There was never any trouble as far as John was concerned. Although Wakefield is not as imposing as Armley, the security is very tight. Visitors have to remove all metal objects and place them in a tray before walking under the security arch.

Any bags or cases have to go under the X-ray machine. I remember one visit in particular. I had purchased a foot pump to use on a small trailer that I was restoring. It was in my work bag under some papers and I had forgotten about it until the the security staff at Wakefield who I might add were extremely professional, quite rightly asked about the strange shape on the X-ray screen. We laughed about what possible uses it could have.

Mobile phones are taboo and have to be left in reception. This is to prevent inamtes making calls that the authorities know nothing about. There are facilities for using telephones in the prison, but they are supervised and limited. Once the prison staff get to know you it is not necessary to show your passport or driving licence when you visit but otherwise, without identification, even lawyers are unable to gain entry.

I found the staff at Wakefield to be helpful and I know of few difficulties at that prison. Being a prison officer is a highly skilled job, as not only do they have to be able to look after themselves, but they have to know and understand the workings of the criminal mind.

After his appearance in the Court of Appeal, John was taken to Hull before discovering that he was to be transferred to Armley as a remand prisoner awaiting trial. Although it had been almost four years since he had left Armley for Wakefield, as soon as he set foot in Armley his old *trouble-maker* tag was firmly attached again and the old problems arose.

There was certainly a *culture shock*. The firm but fair regime at Wakefield, where John felt he was treated with dignity and, particularly since the *Rough Justice* programme, some sympathy, was replaced by the old inmate versus *screw* culture. However this time John knew that within three months he could be a free man.

VIII
Rough Justice

Justice gives sentence many times
On one man for another's crimes.
Samuel Butler (1612–1680)

Having completed the mammoth task of studying the papers, I then had to consider the next move.

Before I could do anything, Shaun contacted me and told me that he had heard that one of the girls who was there on the night of the murder, might be prepared to come forward. He didn't have too many details but promised to let me know if there were any developments. Within the week Shaun was back and I was given the name and address of Stella Harris. This was a most exciting prospect and so I wrote to her in the hope that she would be prepared to see me. I waited for about three weeks, but did not receive a reply. I decided to visit John and see what he could tell me about Stella. He explained that Stella had actually been to see him at the prison and had told him how unhappy she was at the way that the case was proceeding. Like John, she had believed that the Druids were doing everything they could to bring about an appeal and that all would be well. But like John, she too had been misled.

Over the period of time that had elapsed since the case, she had left the Yorkshire area and had settled in Wales.

Away from Sheffield and Rotherham and all her old associates she felt more confident about coming forward.

I decided that the best thing to do would be for me to approach Stella again and find out if she would be willing to make a statement. While preparing to do this I was contacted by a firm of solicitors in Wales, that Stella had visited for advice. It seemed that they were prepared to take a statement from her and send it to me but I took the view that it would be easier if I took the statement based on my knowledge of the case. However, there was a small problem of finance. I could not expect Stella to travel to Rotherham to give me a statement as I already knew that she was unemployed and in receipt of state benefits

I therefore decided that in view of this breakthrough I should approach the Court of Appeal explaining the position and see whether or not they would be prepared to grant me legal aid to travel to Wales and take the statement. I also wondered, if Stella came forward, whether I might be able to persuade her friend Josephine to speak out as well, as I understood that Stella was with Josephine at the time of the murder.

In the meantime, Stella's solicitors sent me a short statement which clearly exonerated John of murder but unfortunately, the statement was incomplete with several points needing clarification and expansion.

I wrote my letter to the Court of Appeal on 4th June 1992, in an attempt to re-open the case.

I received an undated reply shortly afterwards, pointing out that I was the third firm of solicitors who had approached the registrar attempting to secure legal aid for this purpose. I was also told that John himself had written to the court. The registrar replied as follows: ". . . The Single Judge's Directions regarding Legal Aid are quite specific, viz Legal Aid should be confined to Counsel only. You might also be interested to learn that the Registrar exceptionally allowed Counsel, accompanied by a Solicitor, to attend at the Prison for a conference with the Appellant after Leave to Appeal had been granted. Accordingly, I regret that your request for Legal Aid to be extended to yourselves, cannot be acceded to . . ."

We faced a brick wall and I had to make a decision. Should I close my file and say goodbye to the case leaving John to his fate, or continue the case without legal aid and see how far we could get.

There was really no alternative. I believed in the case, and my conscience would never have allowed me to have left the matter as it was, and so I decided to continue.

Even at this stage, John expected the other members of the Druids to come forward. I received a letter from him after one of my prison visits, in which he told me that he had sent a visiting order to Snake (Brian Frankham) which clearly showed that John was still expecting support. However, Frankham had not used it and John was disturbed to find that Frankham had sent two new members who had not been on the Scarborough trip at all.

In the early Summer of 1992 we were under pressure from the Court of Appeal to list the appeal for hearing, but we were not ready. I contacted Andrew Hatton, John's former Junior Counsel and he was extremely helpful when I explained what I was doing. He offered to help by writing to the Court of Appeal in support but John's original appeal had been submitted on the basis of a criticism of the Judge's summing up, suggesting that a full and proper explanation as to provocation had not been put to the jury. In the light of the various developments that had been revealed by my investigations, I did not believe that this was the course to follow.

Mr Hatton told the court in his letter that I was acting for John and was pursuing new witnesses, and therefore, it would be inappropriate to list the appeal until the enquiries were complete and he stated that the early investigations suggested that the appeal, when it was listed would be on different grounds.

The Court of Appeal took notice of Andrew Hatton's communication and did not list the appeal. However, they did not grant legal aid to allow me to find these witnesses, which in my view, avoided any recognition that there was any merit in our case at all.

It was about this time that I was first contacted by Charles Hunter, the Producer of the television programme *Rough Justice*. He had heard about the case on their *grapevine*, and expressed great interest in it. This was one of those strange happenings which played such an important part in our case and which lead me to my first meeting with the BBC.

Some time before, one of my partners, Peter Large, was at a function where he bumped into an old aquaintance from his university days. Peter had studied Law and, I have been told Real Ale at Birmingham University and Nick Wood was a fellow student who he hadn't seen since the day he left.

As many years had passed, they brought each other up to date with their lives since university. Peter explained that he had become a solicitor and was now a partner in the Wilford Smith practice in Rotherham. Nick's life had been a little more interesting as he had taken a job with the BBC and one of the programmes he had worked on was the famous *Rough Justice* programme, which looks into possible miscarriages of justice.

Peter mentioned the Megson case but only in passing and Nick explained that he had already moved onto other things within television. Nevertheless within a few weeks, I received a most interesting telephone call from Charles who told me that he had met Nick Wood who had told him of an interesting case up in Yorkshire. It seems that Nick had paid more attention to what Peter had told him than Peter realized. Unfortunately Nick could not remember the name of the firm Peter worked for, but Charles had heard enough to whet his appetite and it didn't take him long to track me down.

We spoke generally about the case, but bearing in mind the confidentiality with which I have to approach any client's case, I was not able to go into detail. Thankfully, as it turned out, Charles was soon in touch with John who wrote telling me that he had been in communication with Charles Hunter and wished to give his consent for me to talk to the programme. He also wished to waive all confidentiality relating to his case. I had mixed feelings about this, because I knew that courts are very sensitive about how they are portrayed by the media. I also knew that *Rough Justice* was in the business of correcting miscarriages of justice and if they found that the courts had been in any way to blame they would *shout it from the rooftops*.

I therefore didn't want to antagonise the courts in any way which might affect our chances of an appeal but I knew that the publicity *Rough Justice* could bring to the case would put extra pressure on the system to do something.

I decided I would visit John and discuss the implications with him, after which I was convinced that I should speak again to Charles Hunter. John had decided that Charles should have all the case papers from the original trial, which were John's property to do with as he wished.

I let Charles know of John's decision and sent all the papers to London. Within a month, Charles rang and a date was fixed for a meeting between the two of us in Rotherham.

The meeting took place at a local hotel and restaurant called the Brentwood, which I often visit for business lunches and dinners. I found Charles Hunter a complete professional. He had obviously studied all the case papers I had sent him and he accepted that the Megson case was most unusual and he believed that it would make a wonderful programme. We dined extremely well, and at the conclusion of the meeting, we agreed that Charles would have the remaining papers in my possession to photocopy and study. Charles headed back to London with my agreement to keep him fully informed about the progress of the case.

I have since been asked if I thought it was right to work as closely with the producers of the programme as I did and my answer now is the same as it was then. I had absolutely nothing to lose. The Court of Appeal had given us short shrift as regards legal aid and I could not see how we could damage an already closed case any further. It was vital, as I saw it, that we sold the case to *Rough Justice*. They had the financial reserves at their disposal to look fully into this matter, and as they were well versed in the art of investigative journalism, I thought that there was a possibility that they may be able to uncover some new leads. In addition, I was working on the case on a purely voluntary basis and any assistance that I could receive would be greatly appreciated.

There was never any suggestion that I would receive payment from the BBC, either for myself or towards any fund, and indeed I would not have accepted any as I had to preserve our independence so that I was answerable only to my client and not the television company. Charles understood this position and therefore we were able to proceed on a professional and amicable basis. What I demanded in return for my co-operation with them, was the full and frank disclosure of all information that they may obtain in their own investigations. This I received willingly.

I have also been asked, if I thought that the programme tended to sensationalize the case, turning it into a show-biz event. The BBC have to produce programmes that make good television and entertain as well as inform. However, *Rough Justice* is also a programme that is designed to make people think. I believe that their presentation of the Megson case achieved this, and as a result became a very convenient vehicle with which to promote the appeal.

Once again I contacted Andrew Hatton to update him as to the position and in the hope that he would continue to support our appeal.

The Court of Appeal had to be kept informed about all developments, and I thought it best that Andrew should report to the court that we had received a statement from Stella's solicitors which effectively cleared

John of the murder. I also made reference to the involvement of the BBC and suggested that Andrew might also mention this. Although Stella's statement was crucial to the case, I really needed to go into much greater detail with her in a new statement. I had the benefit of seeing all the case papers, and there were a number of questions which remained unanswered, that only I could ask.

As I made arrangements to travel to Wales to meet Stella, I agreed in principle that a member of the *Rough Justice* team be present at the interview, as I could not see my position, or the case being compromised by this. It took some considerable time to set up the meeting at a time convenient for Stella, her solicitor, *Rough Justice* and myself but eventually, we agreed upon a date for the meeting to take place at Stella's own solicitors office.

One afternoon, shortly before the trip to Wales, I received a telephone call the content of which was something of a bomb shell.

I spoke to a man called Mr Kotwal, a pleasant chap from the Court of Appeal office who had obviously seen Mr Hatton's advice letter. He asked me to give a resumé of our progress so far, and in particular the details concerning Stella Harris. At the end of our conversation Mr Kotwal informed me that the Court of Appeal were granting legal aid for me to travel to Wales to obtain an affadavit from Stella Harris. I had also managed to persuade him to allow me to visit Stephen Thomas who at that time was in Lindholme Prison, and to seek out and interview, if possible, Stella's friend Josephine in Chesterfield.

Neither Mr Kotwal nor I referred to the BBC programme, but I have absolutely no doubt that that telephone conversation would not have taken place but for the appearance on the scene of *Rough Justice*.

I immediately wrote to John with the news and made all the arrangements. In addition, I wrote to Josephine asking her to contact me at her convenience. Stephen Thomas who was a former member of the Druids was also considering speaking to me about the trip to the Mere. It seemed that we were at last, starting to get somewhere.

However, Josephine proved to be positively unhelpful. Having read Stella's statement, I knew that Josephine was standing with Stella at the time of the incident and she must have witnessed it. I was therefore keen to get a statement from her, if only to enhance the credibility of Stella's evidence. If I could not get such a statement from Josephine it could only be seen as suspicious and would throw into question the truth of Stella's account. The reply I got from Josephine was as follows:

"Re: Your Letter. Sorry I am not able to phone, as I am working in the daytime and am not able to phone from work.

> I do not think it would be of any help me meeting you to discuss the case as I know of no further information which would help, I stated what I know in my statement.
>
> Sorry I am not able to help any further.
>
> Yours faithfully,
>
> Josephine."

I still did not know Josephine's second name and she clearly wanted nothing to do with us but I realised that I could not expect anything else. She still lived locally with a member of the Druids and had given a false statement to the police. Why should she stick her neck out?

What did surprise me, however, was that just before the Appeal Court hearing Josephine made a statement claiming that Stella could not have seen what she claimed because it was too dark. This was an attempt by the prosecution to discredit Stella's evidence but fortunately, her statement was never used because we were able to discredit it when we discovered that Josephine had lied in an earlier statement to the police.

I had agreed with Mr Kotwal from the Court of Appeal that I would report back with my findings as quickly as possible, because the Court reserved judgement on the question of legal aid thereafter, pending their consideration of such information as I was able to obtain.

Following the disappointment of my contact with Josephine I knew that Stella was to be the most important piece of the jigsaw. So much was going to depend on this meeting. Indeed if I had thought that Stella was a poor witness, or if I had been suspicious that she was not truthful, I would have had to reconsider my position regarding proceeding any further with the case.

She had only made one condition, which was that her own solicitor would be present when she was interviewed. I readily agreed and arrangements were made with Stella's solicitor a most helpful man called Mr Tee from a Colwyn Bay firm of solicitors. I certainly had no objection to him being present as he was a former police officer with considerable experience in criminal law.

IX

Stella Harris

"But now when all was lost or seem'd as lost –
Her stature more than mortal in the burst
Of sunrise, her arm lifted, eyes on fire –
Brake with a blast of trumpets from the gate,
And, falling on them like a thunderbolt.
She trampled some were whelm'd with missiles
of the wall,
And some were push'd with lances from the
rock,
And part were drown'd within the whirling
brook;
O miracle of noble womanhood!"

Tennyson, The Princess

It was a very pleasant August day, when I travelled down to Wales straight after work so that I could have the earliest possible start the following morning.

Although I had previously read Stella's statement there were a number of points I needed to clarify before I could be certain that we had a case.

In our profession, first impressions do count, and when I arrived at the solicitors the following morning, I was told that Stella had been to the office but had left again. I suspected that this meant that she was trying to avoid our meeting, but I was pleased to be proven wrong when she appeared shortly after my arrival. I was introduced to Stella, an attractive lady with a very bubbly personality. She had retained her Yorkshire accent, and this helped us to hit it off immediately.

Within the first few minutes, as we were exchanging memories of various public houses in Rotherham, I had obtained a most favourable impression. Mr. Tee had arranged a room and all the facilities that they could offer and after his secretary had nipped out to get me a bottle of ink, the interview began.

Stella was born in Worksop on 5th June, 1958, and having attended the local state school, left at the age of fifteen to become a stable girl at a local riding school.

Her affinity with animals, particularly horses, made this the perfect job for her and she quickly became an expert horsewoman as well as magnificent in the general day to day running of the stables.

Apart from work, Stella's time was taken up with the motorcycle scene, which is still a very important part of her life. She married at nineteen and within three years had two sons Jamie and Matthew. Unfortunately, the marriage ended in divorce but, she formed a new relationship with one of the members of the Druids called Boggy (Robert Owen). This relationship continued until after John's original trial.

Initially I looked for a motive for her coming forward at this time. I needed answers to the following questions:

1. Why does she want to give evidence?
2. Why has she waited so long to give evidence?

3. What relationship, if any, existed between Megson and herself?

Stella explained that at the time of the murder, she was going out with Boggy (Robert Owen) a member of the Druids and when the case came to court, she was living in Chesterfield, which was well within the area of the Druids group.

She explained that she had two young children and did not wish to place herself or her family in any danger. She had also been told that the Druids were doing everything that they could to secure John's release. All these facts meant that she had kept quiet. This seemed perfectly reasonable behaviour, because if the Druids would be prepared to stab someone for being noisy and playing music too loudly what would they do to a woman who was to *grass* upon the group? I was satisfied with her explanation to my first two questions and so I moved on to her relationship with John. At the time of the incident Stella was going out with a regular boyfriend. She was merely a friend of Megson's through her acquaintance with the other Druid members and there was no other relationship between them. Indeed, after John's sentence there was no contact between them for a long time. Could it be that she had ended her relationship with Boggy and had then wanted to take up with someone else?

I was assured that this was not the case, because her relationship with Boggy had ended a considerable time before, and since then she had had another boyfriend. It seemed quite clear therefore, that there was no relationship other than that which had been explained.

It was clear that Stella was giving evidence because she had realised that the other Druids were not going to help and her conscience had got the better of her. She had also moved to Wales and was in the company of a Welsh biking group who were very supportive and helped to make her feel secure. She emphasized the point that she doubted whether she would have been able to have come forward had she not moved out of the area.

Her explanations seemed reasonable and were ones which I thought any jury would understand. Thus reassured, I recorded her statement with some optimism. The statement I took was as follows:-

> I live at the above address, and have lived in this area for approximately 4 years. Prior to that I lived in Worksop.
>
> Approximately 4 years or so ago, namely 1989, I was associating with a man called Robert with the nickname Boggy.
>
> Boggy was a member of a Sheffield and District Bike Club which had the name of the Druids.
>
> There were a number of members of this particular club and one in particular was a man called John Megson or Mex as he was known. The members of the club were always known by their nicknames and in many cases I did not know their real names and indeed had no cause to do so.
>
> The club held a number of parties and events and used to spend a considerable amount of time travelling around the country attending motorcycle events.
>
> I also knew another member of the Druids who was called Animal. I know that man to be called Colin McCombie. He was married and his wife was also a regular supporter of the Druids.
>
> Animal lived up to his name in that he was an aggressive and particularly unpleasant individual. I have not

had any argument before with this man. I had no personal grievance against him. He was known to carry a knife and indeed I have seen him carrying a knife on occasions.

I had known John Megson because of my relationship with Boggy, and I got on reasonably well with him. We were simply friends by virtue of my relationship with Boggy, but I had no personal relationship with him other than that.

John Megson was a drinking man and he used to drink vodka and coca-cola. It was not unusual for him when we were attending events to drink a lot of this mixture and I have often seen him in drunken states.

From my personal experience with him, he was never aggressive in drink. Indeed, he would often go into his tent and simply sleep it off.

I remember that John Megson was the Vice President of the Druids.

I remember specifically an incident which occurred in 1989 at the Mere in Scarborough in North Yorkshire.

I had gone with a large group of people including my boyfriend Boggy, John Megson and Colin McCombie. There were other people there who I knew by their nick-names and they included people called Yettie, Snake, Junkie and others. There were also some girls present including a friend of mine called Jo (Josephine) and she lives in Chesterfield.

I remember that during the course of the evening, I had some alcohol to drink. I do not drink a lot, because it tends to make me feel sick. I therefore drink within limits.

I remember that during the evening, I saw a lot of John Megson and I remember he was drinking a lot of vodka and coca-cola.

It was my opinion that towards the end of the evening John Megson was very drunk.

I remember during the evening that the group were all situated very close together. We had pitched our tents in a certain area of the park. I remember that various parties had fetched wood for campfires.

I was with John Megson and Boggy for most of the evening.

I remember an incident towards the end of the evening when Animal (Colin McCombie) made some comment about some people who were in a car a distance away. I distinctly remember him being in an aggressive mood and suggesting that he and anyone who would support him should go and *stab them up*. I took that to mean that they should go and pick a fight with them and use a knife.

I think that John Megson was actually in his tent when this was said, but I do remember that one of the group told him not to be so silly and he walked away to another part of our group who sat nearby.

As the evening wore on, John became more and more intoxicated to the extent that I would say he was extremely drunk. He was not in an aggressive mood.

I remember that there were groups of people who were not Druids who were in the area and I remember that some of them were driving past our camp in cars and were shouting. This seemed to upset McCombie who was clearly very aggressive.

When I was with John Megson he did not appear to involve himself in this banter because I was not completely sure that he knew exactly what was going on because of his state.

I remember three lads walked past our particular camp

and one of them was the man Rowley who was later killed.

I remember that one of them appeared to be eating what looked like a Pizza. I believe that he gave a piece of it to one of our group, but I'm not too clear about that.

They were in a tent near to us, although at that particular time I didn't know that, it is only later that I realised that that was the case.

I remember John Megson being on his feet later in the evening and he was walking about. He had difficulty walking because of his drunken state and I particularly remember observing him being on his feet and then either falling against a tent or tripping over one of the tent ropes. He fell into a tent.

The occupants got out and the first out of the tent was the man Rowley. Rowley shouted something to Megson. I cannot remember exactly what was said, but it was in an aggressive tone.

Megson shouted something back, but it wasn't clear what he said, and the next thing I knew was that the man Rowley hit Megson. Megson started to scuffle with the youth. I did not see anything in Megson's hand. I know that Megson did not carry a knife.

Megson then appeared to be having difficulties in the struggle and Colin McCombie came on the scene. I don't know where he came from or what direction he came from.

He (McCombie) then twisted him (Rowley) round and had him by the neck. Rowley's back was to McCombie's front. McCombie then appeared to punch this lad in the back. He then swivelled him round and I saw his hand go towards Rowley's front, although it was partially obscured by McCombie's body.

I could not see whether McCombie had anything in his hand at that stage, but I was particularly struck by the way that Rowley's legs just appeared to go. He lost all use of his legs and started to fall.

As McCombie was doing this, Megson was a pace or two away and did not have any contact with Rowley when McCombie was fighting with him.

As Rowley started to fall, he fell into Megson and immediately knocked Megson to the floor and fell upon him. I cannot say exactly where he was laid on Megson whether it was to his left, right or all the way across his body, but certainly it was Rowley's fall that knocked Megson to the floor.

Megson went literally straight to the floor and made no attempt to either dodge Rowley or side step him.

I then saw McCombie, the man called Snake (Brian Frankham) and some of the other men start to kick Rowley and indeed they literally kicked him off Megson.

Megson remained on the ground and it wasn't clear whether he was conscious or not.

The lad was kicked off Megson as I have said and those kicks moved him a short distance away. This was into the area of a thicket and it was dark there and I couldn't exactly see what was happening.

Jo was with me at the time and I remember saying to her 'he's dead'. I distinctly remember the way that the lad fell onto Megson and his legs going as I had described. It was obvious to me that the worst had happened. I think that one of them picked John up. He certainly helped John back towards the tent. I remember that he (Megson) had a cut on his mouth where Rowley had hit him.

We were back at the tent when a very short time later

McCombie appeared on the scene. He was carrying a knife which was blood stained. I have no doubt about that. He wiped the knife on the grass. He then announced that if he put the knife into the fire it would remove all traces of blood.

It was a black handled knife about six inches in total length. I saw him put it into the fire for a short period. He then took the knife and left the area of the tent. When he returned, he did not have the knife.

At the time, he was wearing a heavy leather jacket.

I remember that we went into our respective tents, but there had been a discussion as to whether we should stay or go.

We stayed the night, but the following morning the police had cordoned off the entire area.

I was taken to the police Station and I was put into a big room with others. I was terrified at the time.

I admit that I told the police that I had seen nothing.

I was terrified of McCombie and was frightened to grass anybody in the incident. I thought that the arrangement was that nobody would admit anything. If anyone should be wrongly charged with the matter involving Rowley, then the guilty party would own up to the police.

I would add that I did not take part in the incident but I did watch it, I did nothing to try to stop it, but there was nothing I could do.

When I was released by the police I eventually went home.

I was present at one or two meetings thereafter of the club and I distinctly remember McCombie making it quite clear that nobody had to say anything.

When Megson was charged with murder, I wanted to

do something about it but I had to admit that I was terrified.

McCombie was known to live up to his nickname. He had no conscience or scruples and everyone feared him because he was so dangerous.

The club began to break up as a result of this incident and I broke up my association with Boggy.

I simply wanted to get out of the area and so I left and came to Wales.

I have stayed here ever since.

I have thought about this case since the time that John Megson was sent to prison and I have always wanted to say something and do something, but quite frankly I have been too frightened. If McCombie was prepared to stab someone who he didn't know, he would be more than prepared to stab someone if he thought that they were going to get him into trouble.

About a year ago, I decided to write to John Megson and we have corresponded.

I became aware that he was represented by a solicitor who was pushing for an appeal.

After a great deal of soul searching, I decided that I would make myself available as a witness, although I am in fear.

I then understood that other members of the group were going to come forward and this assisted my resolve to put matters right.

John's solicitor acquired my address and wrote to me with a view to taking a statement.

I was concerned about the matter but wanted to see justice done. Consequently I sought advice from a local solicitor with a view to arrangements being made to take a statement from me.

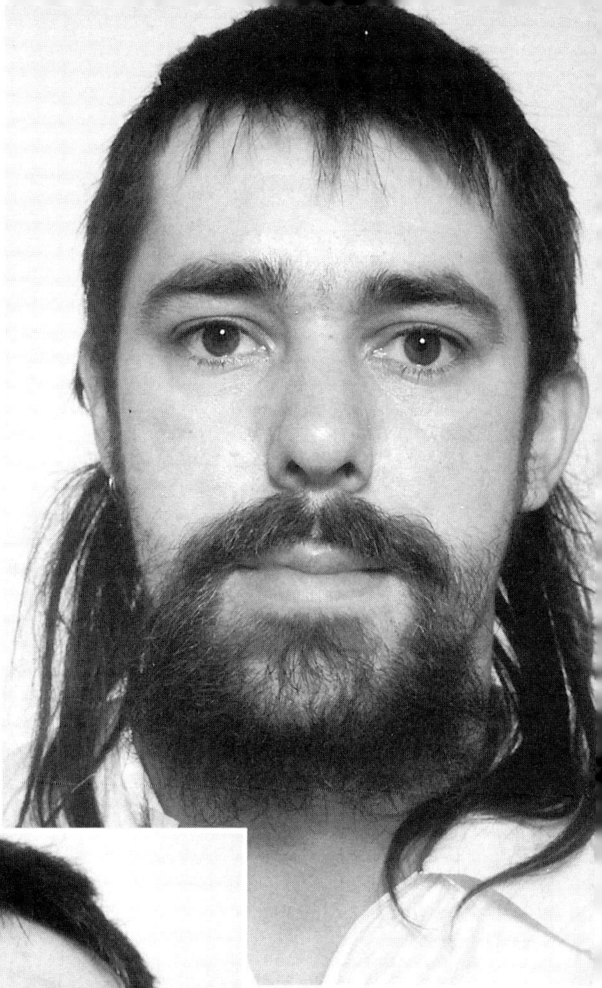

John Megson photographed by police photographer on Sunday 23rd April 1989. Note the yellow police issue overall given to Megson when his clothes were taken for forensic testing.

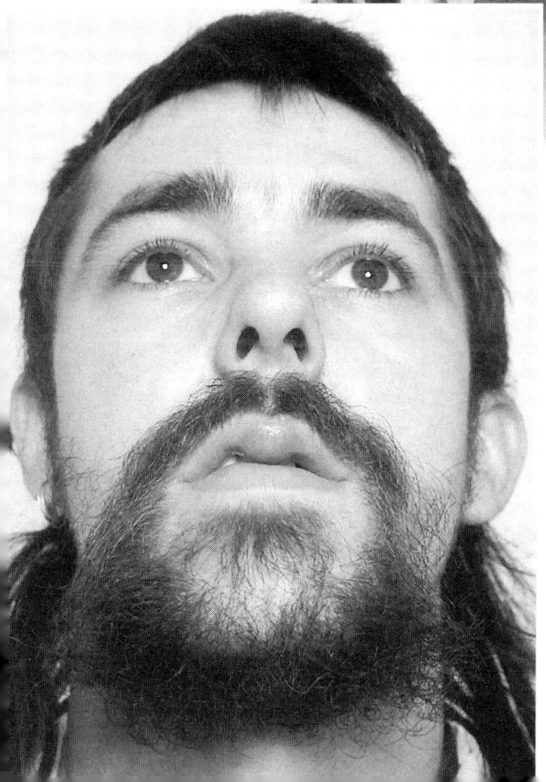

John Megson with head raised for police photographer to show his swollen lip believed to have been caused by Stephen Rowley after Megson had fallen onto the tent Rowley was sleeping in.

View of Scarborough Mere taken from the perimeter road the day after Rowley's murder.

The day after the murder many bikers were still encamped around the Mere. Most of them had been unaware of any of the events surrounding the stabbing.

The site of the Rowley, Lynn, Drakesmith and Richardson encampment showing the tent and Neil Drakesmith's Volkswagen Golf.

The partially collapsed tent onto which a drunken Megson had fallen and out of which Rowley clambered to meet his death.

Front (above) and rear (below) of Druids' Clubhouse in Fitzwilliam Road Rotherham as it was in April 1989.

Interior of the Druids' Clubhouse. Above: The room in which the Druids met to agree the story that would be given to the police and in which Rowley's murderer confessed his crime.
Below: The Clubhouse bar boasting that the Druids did not regard themselves as among the 99% of law-abiding bikers.

Saturday May 18th 1994: The day after John Megson's release.

Top left: John with the three people who knew he hadn't done it.

Top right: John and Stella with everything to smile about.

Bottom left: John in thoughtful mood. "It's hard to talk about because a 19 year old lad died. It's good to be out but no matter how good it is for us, what's his family thinking? There's a geezer out there that has killed their son."

The wedding at Abergele Registry Office, North Wales, 3rd September 1994. Below: "The fight for my freedom taught me to trust and believe in people again: in a woman who put her very life at risk to right a wrong done to a friend, and in a man who put his reputation and wallet on the line for justice." John Megson in his foreword to "Hell is not for Angels", Jan 1997.

Colin (Animal) McCombie during the final trial. He was found guilty of Manslaughter but has justice been done?

Simon (Yettie) Negrotti during the final trial. He was also found guilty of Manslaughter.

As a result of this, information as to what I proposed leaked to members and former members of the Druids.

My address was not known to the Druids but I understand that they have found out that I was associating with a biker in Wales. Christopher Owen was contacted by Snake (Brian Frankham). He said that he wanted to see me about that matter.

I agreed to see him at an independent address with some of my Welsh biker friends present. I was told that if I saw him there would be no trouble.

I knew Snake to be a friend of John Megson or rather he was at the time of the incident.

I saw him by arrangement, he was accompanied by Geordie and Yettie.

We had a conversation about John Megson. The effect of the conversation was that Snake did not want me to make a statement. He wanted me to leave things as they were because if I was to make a statement as to what happened, it would get other people into trouble who had escaped charges so far.

He was not nasty to me and he didn't threaten me but then he wouldn't have done so in the presence of my friends.

He kept trying to persuade me to keep quiet.

I pointed out that I had agreed to tell the truth about the incident and had committed myself to so doing. Snake then tried to persuade me to keep to my original story and leave things as they were. I refused and told him that he had to stand and be counted. I meant by this that he should say what really happened.

He kept saying that they all had a lot to lose. I told him that my mind was made up and the truth would have to come out regardless of the consequences. The meeting took place in April 1993.

I still associate with my boyfriend and did not and do not have a relationship with John Megson other than I have described.

I very much regret not taking action earlier but I was frightened, I still am but I feel much safer now that I have the support of the club in Wales. Snake was told at the meeting I had with him, that they supported me and would stand by me. So far as I am aware, John Megson has no contact with my friends who have no axe to grind and do not favour any party in this matter, but I have been taken to the prison by Stuart Dawson and Dino, who came into the prison with me.

In addition, I spoke to Jo who I have referred to above, and she intends to come forward to make a statement. I worry for her because she lives in Yorkshire and will clearly place herself at risk in coming forward.

I wish that I had had the courage to do so myself, but a lot earlier than this.

Signed Stella Harris

Stella did not question me carefully upon what was to happen, which I found consistent with someone who had told me the truth and got the story off her chest as opposed to someone who had a direct motive for telling lies.

I thanked Stella for her help and told her how brave she had been. I shook hands with Mr. Tee and I was in good spirits as I set off on my way back to Yorkshire.

I decided to take a sentimental journey home, because I remembered visits to North Wales as a child. My parents always or nearly always took my brother and me to North Wales for our annual holiday. It was fairly easy to get to even in the late fifties and early sixties, and it was unheard of for anyone from our locality to go abroad in those days. The only aeroplane I had seen close to, was the Spitfire that I had made from an Airfix kit.

I decided to drive into Colwyn Bay itself and on the way back to visit Prestatyn where we used to stay at a boarding house. We would play on the beach every day and every day was hot and the sun never stopped shining.

I stopped the car on the sea front and had climbed out and gone down the steps to stand on the beach before I realized that the sun was not shining. It was cold, wet and windy and I was stood in pinstripe trousers and white shirt and tie. My shirt was quickly becoming skin-coloured as the rain stuck the white cotton to my already shivering body. Then I saw a local fisherman in his oilskins, digging for worms. He must have thought that I was someone from the local mental hospital as I stood there on the beach looking out to sea dressed as I was, particularly when I laughed out loud as I recalled some of those memories from the past. He moved further down the beach keeping me in view in case I made any sudden movements.

I remembered one day when my father had pushed my brother and me into the sea for a swim. The sea was freezing cold and yet he urged us on. I couldn't help thinking that if the social services knew of any parent doing that now, with two young lads with proclivities to bronchitis, we would have been snatched into care immediately. How odd it was that parents deemed such torture beneficial for their children.However, we were willing participants and enjoyed every minute of it, especially when we removed the ice from our swimming trunks.

I also remembered when we left the beach for the last time before going home. My brother who was younger than me, would turn to the sea and say his goodbyes until the next time.

This time, I turned to walk back up the beach to the car and didn't look back.

By the time I got into the car I was soaking wet with rain and sea mist. As I drove off the fisherman looked at me shaking his head, so I opened the window and waved to him. He waved back using both his fingers.

I then tried to find a place called Llanddulas. I remember on my last trip there with my parents, we had travelled on my father's motorcycle and side car. My father loved motorcycles and the only compromise he made for my mother was to fit it with a side car. It was a 650 cc BSA Gold Flash and my experiences of that bike and the knowledge of all the great names of the golden years of the British motorcycle industry that I learned from my father, were to be beneficial much later when I met John Megson and his biking companions.

Many years before, when we had ridden up Llanddulas Hill, something happened to the motorcycle and the engine caught fire. My father was driving and I was sitting on the pillion. My mother was in the front of the side car and my younger brother was sitting in the little seat behind her. When we got to the Llanddulas Church the engine set alight and local road sweepers helped to put it out. My father was less than pleased and gave full verve to a magnificent range of expletives. It was throwing it down with rain and we sheltered in the archway which was the entrance to both the cemetery and church grounds.

Fortunately, my father was a member of the Automobile Association and they were soon on the scene to repair the damage. I had my sandwiches that day in Llanddulas Cemetery. We went there because my father thought that it would be a good idea to visit the local museum which housed cars belonging to Hitler and Mussolini. My father thought that that might entertain my brother and me, although I can't for the life of me think why.

Trying to find it, I became lost which is not unusual for me on foreign soil and I stopped one of the locals and asked him for directions to the cemetery. It transpired that he was on holiday and he was looking for the Museum so that he could see the Hitler and Mussolini cars, so I gave it up as a bad job and drove on.

Within a very short distance, I came to a hill which led to the church and cemetery. I had found the old place quite by chance, just as it began to rain again. It was just as I remembered it, with its beautiful old church, the cemetery and the gateway entrance. I thought it strange that such a place would fascinate me, but it was obviously important to me as a child and that is why it stood out in my mind. I stayed for a minute or two and then went on my way.

I had all but completed my sentimental journey and decided that my route back would take me through the town of Rhyl. It was closed when I got there and I was thankful for that. Surely this could not be the place that we visited every year. I realized that not only do places change, but so do people. They grow up of course and what would entrance a child might not even interest an adult, but I enjoyed the memories and turned for home.

I took a wrong turning and instead of finding the motorway, I ended up in a traffic jam in a godforsaken place called Flint. As I was in the queue, I noticed a man sitting on a bench by the side of the road. He was in his fifties, overweight, sweating profusely and wearing brand new running shoes, shorts and shirt. What on earth possessed a man his age and weight to run around? I wound the window down and shouted across to him, but he was too tired to get up from the bench. I asked him for the motorway, but he was unable to answer and just gave a series of gesticulations.

Following the route as best I could, I made very little progress over the next ten minutes and sure enough as I waited in the stream of traffic, who should come hobbling past but *Steve Ovett* whose beer belly was wobbling at such a rate that it must have totally congealed all the previous weeks boozing.

He stopped at the car, realizing that he had not been too helpful at our last meeting. He was in a very breathless state and as best he could, he gave me certain directions and with that he ran off.

I followed the directions to the letter, winding around a number of back roads to find very much to my chagrin, that I had ended up back in the traffic jam again at the entrance to Flint. I decided that if I saw the *marathon man* again, I would run him over. Unfortunately, I didn't see him, and I presumed he had either completed his journey or the ambulance had taken him away.

I eventually found my way to Chester and from Chester to the motorway and home. The next day was Sunday and in the afternoon I decided to dictate a full statement from my notes while it was fresh in my memory. It took some considerable time and I recorded it as best I could. Bearing in mind the importance of this statement, I thought it right to send a copy to Mr. Tee and ask him if he could go though it with Stella altering it if necessary and return it to me.

It was returned within four or five days with one or two alterations. I sent an amended copy to be signed and witnessed and it was returned expeditiously.

I had arranged by that time to see Stephen Thomas at Lindholme. Stephen Thomas was later to appear in the *Rough Justice* television programme, but his name had been given to me by John as being a supporter and someone who might be able to help our case.

I travelled to Lindholme, a prison some thirty miles from Rotherham, for our appointment.

Mr. Thomas reminded me that I had acted for a lad called Christopher Beverington on a road traffic case some years before and he had been one of the witnesses. I remembered the case and he was surprised by the detail I was able to recall. In particular I remembered a bright orange helmet which was a feature of the identification evidence and Mr. Thomas appeared to be suitably impressed. Having achieved that degree of rapport, we turned to the business in hand.

However, Mr. Thomas had not been in Scarborough on the night of the incident and was therefore unable to help me with any direct evidence at all. He did tell me, however, that he did not believe for one minute that John Megson had inflicted the wounds that led to Mr. Rowley's death. We discussed the case and Mr. Thomas did his best to give what information he could without compromising himself with the Druids.

It seemed unlikely that he would be able to help by way

of direct evidence and consequently the meeting came to an end and I set off back to Rotherham. Later Stephen Thomas was to be particularly brave when he agreed to appear on the *Rough Justice* programme to explain some of the events surrounding the post-Scarborough run meetings and the lead up to the trial.

I prepared the documentation for submission to the Court of Appeal and sent them by first class post. I had taken the opportunity of asking my friend Alan Goldsack Q.C. his views before sending them. As ever he was most careful and concise in his judgement but the gist of it was that he thought that we were in with a chance.

In submitting the documents, I invited the Court of Appeal to extend my legal aid certificate to cover the instructing of Counsel to advise on the merits of an appeal. A member of the Court of Appeal staff contacted me by telephone shortly after the statements had been delivered and suggested that legal aid might be extended for that purpose but I had to use the original Counsel.

I explained to him that I took the view that it would be better for a fresh mind on the subject and that I wished to instruct Alan Goldsack Q.C. I indicated that he had been kind enough to give me advice on the matter already without being briefed and I felt that it was in the interests of justice to instruct someone else.

The staff at the Court of Appeal were keen to explain the economic exercise that they apply to cases of this sort.

I expressed a view that economic considerations were probably inappropriate in this particular case bearing in mind its history and not to put too fine a point on it, I was quite insistent. I was left to make written representations which I did. The Court of Appeal were under a great deal of pressure to resolve this long standing matter and I finally managed to persuade them that this was a case for fresh Counsel. I set about briefing Alan Goldsack Q.C. who already had the benefit of knowing the background to the case. I prepared the various documents and submitted them to him and with his usual speed and vigour he prepared a written advice.

His recommendations were that the previous grounds of appeal should be abandoned and the Court should consider granting leave to appeal on the grounds that there was new evidence which the court should consider.

The first hurdle was to persuade the Court of Appeal that we should get a hearing for the court to consider whether we could have leave to bring the new evidence. The hearing would take the form of an application for permission to bring our appeal on the basis of Stella's statement.

At that time, Alan Goldsack was prosecuting a very serious fraud case in Leicester and this was taking up a considerable amount of his time. Nevertheless, he faxed me the advice and new grounds of appeal which I submitted the next day.

It was only a matter of a fortnight or so before we received confirmation that the Court of Appeal would hear the application on Friday 22nd February 1994. There was no argument about the date. We were told that that was the date we were given and no other would be agreed.

In the documents I received, it was not clear whether or not just the application for leave would be heard, or whether in fact the court would require us to call our new evidence for them to consider as well. Alan Goldsack's clerk very helpfully checked with the Court of Appeal to see what was in their mind and it became quite obvious to me that if leave was granted they would expect us to call the evidence before the court.

This did not leave me a great deal of time to make all the necessary arrangements. Stella would be required to give evidence so I set about arranging for her attendance. I should add, that legal aid had been granted, but disappointingly had been limited to Leading Counsel only and this meant that Alan Goldsack would be on his own and would not have the assistance of a Junior to do a lot of the leg work. I thought this rather unfair because the prosecution had the benefit of two Counsel and as this was substantially a defence application on a very serious point, then I would have thought that we ought to have been allowed that same facility.

The Court of Appeal was intransigent on this point, although I got the distinct impression later at the hearing itself that Lord Justice Glidewell, the presiding judge in the application for leave was rather surprised to find only Leading Counsel and no Junior.

I reported the position to John and then to his family and of course to Stella who was the substance of our case. She was not on the telephone, so it was difficult to ensure that she had received our letter, but we used a *jungle drum* type link that was to telephone one of Stella's friends and a message would be given to her. It was an unusual state of affairs, but one that I had to put up with. I eventually managed to make contact with Stella who confirmed her availability and I quickly arranged a meeting with Shaun to explain in more detail what had gone on.

The other reason for the meeting was to try to keep his feet firmly on the ground, because while it seemed that we were making some progress, I didn't want Shaun to get too carried away because it would be a simple matter for the Court of Appeal to say no. I also reported the position to the members of the *Rough Justice* team, because they clearly had an interest in the matter and it would have been less than courteous not to inform them.

This placed a great deal of pressure on them, because their programme would have to be finished and transmitted before the Court of Appeal hearing date.

Arrangements were put in hand for the final bits of filming.

The BBC told me that they would require my attendance and wanted me to deal with a number of legal points in front of the cameras. I was happy to assist, but I had to bear in mind that I could not say anything that would compromise the case. I was really in two minds as to what to say and so, over the next few days, I gave the matter much thought. The *Rough Justice* team were anxious to trace the whereabouts of the other members of the Druids and they asked me for the name of a local private investigator who would be able to carry out this task. I suggested John Bradwell, an ex-police officer with many years experience. A meeting was arranged at my office which John attended and Charles Hunter informed me of his requirements. Fortunately, the BBC picked up his bill because John's services do not come cheaply but he does get results.

The BBC crew were to start filming on the Thursday. All the schedules had been worked out and they would to start at Shaun's house in the morning, with my section to follow after lunch.

X

Rough Justice and the Code of Silence

> O purblind race of miserable men,
> How many among us at this very hour
> Do forge a lifelong trouble for ourselves,
> By taking true for false, or false for true;
> Here, thro' the feeble twilight of this world
> Groping, how many, until we pass and reach
> That other where we see as we are seen!
>
> *Tennyson*, Idylls of the King

On the Thursday morning I received a telephone call from Shaun to say that the BBC had arrived but were a little late and shortly after that, Charles Hunter, the producer of *Rough Justice*, telephoned to tell me that our meeting would take place an hour later than had been arranged. I set about thinking what I wanted to say, only too aware that as the BBC would have fairly definite views about what they would want to ask. Charles Hunter arrived at 12.15 pm, together with John Ware who was to be the presenter of the programme. I had not met John before and I was keen to discuss the points he would want me to deal with. John was a smart executive type with a shock of grey hair, and it was easy to see why he was a BBC presenter.

Charles inspected our office for the most appropriate vantage point for filming. The camera crew followed fairly soon after but David Odd, the senior cameraman felt that our interviewing rooms were too small for his purpose. It was time for lunch in any event so we set off for the local Chinese restaurant at the BBC's invitation. As we ate the sweet and sour we discussed the afternoon's filming. I was given a broad description of what was required of me and John Ware and I discussed the case on a fairly general basis. Apparently Shaun's interview had gone extremely well and according to what Charles told me, Shaun did not mince his words making fairly frequent use of expletives where he thought it appropriate. Nevertheless, Charles felt that Shaun came over as being genuine. They had taken a lot of film, but it would have to be edited down to fit in with the time schedule for the programme.

I knew that television programmes involved an enormous amount of work and preparation time but until I actually took part, I didn't realize the full extent of it. I was surprised to see how many people were involved even in the shooting of a single interview like mine, but I soon understood how necessary they all were.

The full crew consisted of the following:

The Producer;
The Assistant Producer;
The Director;
The Cameraman;
The Lighting Man;
The Sound Man;

The Presenter/Interviewer;
and all of them had an integral part to play. After lunch we returned to the office so that the cameraman could have another look.

The sight of the cameras thrilled our waiting-room full of clients and one of my regulars, Alec Walker apparently had a bet with one of the other clients that he could get in on the filming as an *extra*.

I later found out that he had bet that he would be able to engineer himself a *walking on part*. In this he failed because his bit ended up on the cutting-room floor and even to this day he is being pursued for the £5!

I hit on the idea of using the local Rotherham Club as a location since this is a private members' club where many of the local business community gather. It has a very large room with an *olde worlde* look enhanced by seasoned leather armchairs and a signed picture of Winston Churchill on one of the walls. David Odd, the cameraman, thought that the room was excellent and I arranged with the steward to use it. The crew promptly set about re-arranging the entire club and I soon realized that when the general public think there is going to be some filming done they bend over backwards to assist in the hope that they might get on the box. As it is unusual and interesting to watch, people are often wooed by such prospects and the television people get to use premises as their own.

A suitable chair was picked out for my interview and I promptly disappeared to the lavatory to do my hair. At this point I looked a little off-colour but I was assured by the cameraman that they could colour my cheeks in when they came to edit the film.

I was intrigued to learn the various terms that were

used for the respective camera angles and interviewing techniques. At the end of the day's filming when I explained what had happened to my colleagues I made considerable use of the terms *one shot*, *two shot* and the like. I was not given any form of run-through because Charles felt that the interview should come over as being general conversation and unprepared.

They got what they wanted, because I wasn't prepared. I make my living standing up in public and discussing cases and to that extent having an audience did not perturb me but I have to confess to being a little less than happy at being interviewed on camera. You are very much aware of the fact that you are surrounded by people watching and noting your every move and it is fair to say that my initial comments were not as good as I thought they should have been because I felt inhibited by the presence of the camera. We did a second take by which time I was more comfortable and was getting used to the presence of the cameras.

There was a lot of pressure upon me at that time as I did not want to let the programme down and was concerned about what people would think of my performance. Perhaps most importantly, I had a considerable fear of saying something in an unguarded moment which might have prejudiced the case.

I lightened the atmosphere by telling the company about an incident in one of the local courts which had happened to me a week or so before. My case had been called on and it involved two defendants but only one of them had turned up.

"Where's your co-accused?" boomed one of the magistrates with the air of a man who had allowed the position to go to his head.

"What's a co-accused?" asked the defendant pathetically.

"Ask him where he is," said the magistrate. I leaned across from my bench to the dock and asked where the unfortunate Mr. Roddiskowski was. That's why he called him *Co-accused* I thought to myself. Who has a name like Roddiskowski? The defendant present was called Jones. What a contrast?

I really didn't think that it was my job to enquire after someone I didn't represent but out of respect for the court I made the enquiry. At the time, I was suffering from an excess of ear wax, a problem that has followed me since childhood. It meant that I was unable to pick up a whispered answer. "Where is he?" I asked.

"Not here," came the reply.

"I can see that," I said indignantly.

"But why isn't he here?"

"He's got nits," came the reply.

"Nits." I thought that is peculiar but I reported the position to the magistrate who was totally dissatisfied with the explanation which he made clear when he announced,

"But Mr. Smith, people don't fail to attend because of nits, that doesn't stop someone from attending court. Check it!"

I was trying to fill in my case log and so I wasn't too pleased at having to jump up and down like a yo-yo but I did check again. This time I heard what he said "I'm sorry sir," I announced with as much regret as I could muster, "I misheard him. He said he's suffering from gastroenteritis, but don't ask him to spell it."

By this time the equipment was being packed away, and I returned to the office with Charles and John.

Kate, my Secretary, prepared some tea and we discussed the day's filming. "It's in the can," said Charles.

"Oh I rather hope not," said I, having placed a different connotation on the word *can.* It wasn't long before they were on their way to film the other members of the Druids; a clear indication that when the BBC set out to do a thing, they don't mess about. I thought it would be dangerous to tackle them but experience must have taught the BBC how far they can go. I didn't know at that time what they intended to do and I certainly didn't know that they had a secret camera!

Shortly before the transmission in January 1994, I arranged to visit the BBC at the Television Centre in London. I wanted to see if there was anything on the film that Rough Justice had obtained which I could use in the case. After all, they had access to substantial funds which had been put to good use in clever preparation and Charles informed me that they had obtained some interesting material which I couldn't wait to see.

On the due date, I arrived at Doncaster station and walked on to the platform. As I waited, I was filled with expectations, luxuriating in the positive delights of being away from the usual day down at the magistrate's court. I enjoy work, but the daily grind can be quite exacting and the opportunity to have a day out of court is always most welcome.

One of the difficulties we have as advocates, is that our clients tend to expect us to be at their beck and call and, because many of them are criminals, although I hasten to add not all, have little concern for our welfare. By their very nature they are extremely self-centred people who care little for the convenience or comfort of others.

I arrived in London at approximately 10.30 am which left me ample time to take a very leisurely journey to the Television Centre.

I have always been fascinated by the various sights in a tube station where there is always plenty of entertainment with the buskers and weird characters that you see on your way. I couldn't help thinking how times had changed since my early visits to London in the sixties. The place was now burdened with beggars but I got through the station unscathed and entered the tube train.

It delivered me to within walking distance of the BBC Television Centre. I was rather surprised at the area, because it was generally less than impressive apart from the Television Centre itself and I imagined that it was not the most pleasant place to walk at night. I walked to the welcome desk, to see that there was a high degree of security, ensuring that one simply could not gain admittance without an appointment.

Fortunately, they found my name on the visitors' list for the day and I was shown to a waiting room until I was directed to the meeting place within the main building.

I was looking forward to this visit and I was not disappointed when Irene McMillan arrived to take me to the BBC restaurant for lunch where Charles and Margaret Penn, the assistant producer joined us.

We sat down to an excellent lunch while Charles explained to me that they had managed to film the Druids, but didn't give me the exact details because I was to witness the real thing in the editing room later.

After coffee, we went to the department where the film was being prepared and I met Howard Billingham, the film editor supervising all the attention that was being given to the film. The first step was to make a video tape from the original film and work with that. By using sophisticated computerized equipment, Howard was able to alter the light and colour of the film and to perform all manner of wizardry with the tape. I asked him if he could make me look thinner and younger but he explained that it was a computer and not Merlin's cave so I had to be content with a little soft-focus to remove some of the railway lines from my forehead.

I was able to watch the tape time after time while Howard achieved the improvements he wanted and the finished article was stored on a large film wheel on the computer. I was treated to a real surprise when the film of the Druids arrived on screen. I was astonished by it. How on earth did they manage to film them? Charles soon explained how they had used a secret camera but enquire as I might, he refused to tell me exactly how it was done.

Seeing my own interview, I said to the group which had gathered in the editing room "He's a good looking lad!" "Rubbish," came the reply and perhaps that summed up my performance. On reflection, I don't think I did too badly but unless you've undergone an interview like that, you simply don't realize how difficult it is. I picked up some interesting points which I thought would be of some use and generally I was extremely happy with what I saw. I was to be even happier with the finished article when the programme was relayed in February 1994.

The video tape included a number of interviews and comments from John Ware together with a brilliantly filmed reconstruction of the incident itself at the Mere.

For this purpose a number of actors were selected to play the parts of the Druids and their girlfriends and I found that the actors were very true to the characters they had to portray. The BBC costume department had prepared the outfits and a special crew had lit bonfires around the Mere. The exact locations were used as Stella Harris had helped to select them and to add to the authenticity, filming took place very late at night. The BBC stores department provided tents, uniforms, motorcycles and even a police van. Other location shots included visits to Wakefield, Armley Prison Leeds and my office in sunny Rotherham. The overall effect was an intriguing film full of thought provoking material.

Charles and I left Howard to continue with his work and we set off across London to visit the *Rough Justice* office where the team was busy at work on another case. Charles explained how rigorous the vetting procedure had to be in order to protect the excellent reputation the programme had established. Most initial enquiries begin with a letter from a defendent who then allows the team access to his case papers. These are then studied at which point most of them are politely turned down. However a number do get through to be developed into a project for *Rough Justice*. Charles told me of one case which had passed all the vetting procedures and production work had been well under way when the team had discovered that the man at the centre of the case was, in fact, guilty. Charles could do nothing but drop the case. He went on to talk about many of the successes the team had over the years but stressed that the John Megson story was one of the most interesting and important cases they had yet dealt with.

Having been involved in ony a small part of the filming, but having watched the editing and the office at work, I realised just how much time and effort goes into a programme of this kind. The viewer would see just forty minutes on screen but what they wouldn't see would be the hours of filming that would be left *on the cutting room floor*.

At about 6 pm I thanked Charles for a most interesting and instructive day and caught a taxi to Kings Cross station. By 7 pm I was on my way home pouring my thoughts into my dictaphone in an attempt to record everything I had seen and heard. I had arranged to brief Alan Goldsack on my findings and although the programme was to go out in less than three weeks, many of my initial concerns about the media involvement had been removed.

There was the usual list of telephone messages when I got back to the office one of which was from Steve Caddy of the Sheffield and Rotherham Star. He had received a BBC press release about the programme and wanted my story. I rang him back to fill in some details but honoured my promise to Charles not to mention the secret filming of the Druids.

On the 25th January 1994 Shaun Megson and I met at the BBC Radio Sheffield office in Broomhill, Sheffield. We had agreed to appear on the Breakfast Show in order to let local people know that the following evening's *Rough Justice* programme on BBC1 was about a local man. We were given cups of coffee before being taken straight into the studio while a record was being played. The record, Elvis Presley's *Jailhouse Rock* seemed strangely appropriate. We met the presenter, Mia Webb as she got on with her morning show which was a mixture of records, guests, announcements and general chit-chat. Shaun and I were to be her guests for that morning and without any rehearsal we were introduced to the listeners and Mia began putting questions to us. I tended to deal with the legal issues and Shaun talked about how the case had affected the Megson family. We were *on air* for about twenty minutes and I was surprised at how many people let me know that they had heard the broadcast.

However, the following night many millions more would know of the John Megson case when *Rough Justice: Code of Silence* was broadcast on BBC1 at 9.30 pm prime time. The next day I appeared in Sheffield Court, where I knew I would have to withstand a barrage of witty comments about my performance on TV. Preparing to give as good as I got, I was completely thrown by what one of the solicitors said to me. "I saw the programme last night and I have to say that I thought you were brilliant." I was astonished as he appeared to be quite genuine.

"Well . . . thank you . . . I . . ." I didn't know what to say but he interrupted my stuttered thanks.

"Yes. I loved the bit where you were throwing around the cans of beer. It was marvellous!"

I had been had! He was referring to the re-enactment scene in the programme where actors dressed as scruffy, bearded bikers indulged in drunken loutish behaviour. We both laughed and I told him to "Sod Off'.

By the time I returned to the office I had heard every possible witty remark about the programme at least five times. But I was still able to telephone Charles Hunter and congratulate him on a job well done before tackling an even longer than usual list of telephone messages which this time were mostly about the programme.

The next day I was in the Rotherham Court about to deal with a mitigation when someone tapped me on the shoulder and said, "Your make-up is running." I turned round to him and replied.

"Yes. But is my wig straight?" Such is the price of fame for a day.

XI

The Court of Appeal

> Be true, if you would be believed. Let a man but speak forth with genuine earnestness the thought, the emotion, the actual condition of his own heart; and other men, so strangely are we all knit together by the tie of sympathy, must and will give heed to him.
>
> *Thomas Carlyle*

The Court of Appeal hearing was less than a month after the *Rough Justice* television transmission so there was no time to bask in the glory of seeing myself on national television. There was still much work to be done.

Stella's statement was to be the crucial piece of evidence in support of the appeal and with Josephine refusing to offer corroborative evidence I knew there was a weak point in our case which the prosecution would certainly attack. We discovered that when the police had seen Stella's statement, which had been submitted to the Court of Appeal, they had checked every detail. They then went to see Josephine and asked her if she had seen the murder.

To have agreed with Stella's statement would have

implicated her in the *Code of Silence* and placed her at the scene of the murder. This would have meant that she had given a false statement to the police when the Druids were taken into Scarborough police station on the day of the murder as she had claimed to have seen nothing. Not surprisingly therefore she made a statement absolving herself from all responsibility. When asked to comment on Stella's statement she had no option but to say that Stella was lying and could not have seen what she had claimed.

We were told of this development by the prosecution who saw it as the way to destroy the credibility of Stella's statement. I knew that they intended to use it at the appeal court hearing but could see no way of stopping them casting doubt on Stella's truthfulness.

It was at this point if no other when my agreeing to work with the *Rough Justice* team really paid off. I told Charles Hunter of my concern about Josephine's statement and he immediately told me that he had needed to satisfy himself that Stella was telling the truth and knowing Josephine was unwilling to help, he had set up a telephone conversation between the two women which had been recorded. In the conversation Stella had tried to get Josephine to tell the truth but she didn't want to get involved. This was understandable to a certain extent as she was still with Nick (Nicholas Woodhead) and lived in the locality. However, a number of things Josephine said including mention of the meetings in the clubhouse after the murder were in direct conflict with her statement. The tape was dynamite.

When Martin Bethel Q.C. put Josephine's statement to Alan Goldsack before the Court of Appeal hearing, he must have thought he had destroyed our case even before we got into court. Alan's response was to tell him of the BBC tape and allow him to see the relevant part of the transcript. As a result the prosecution did not call Josephine, leaving them with little with which to attack Stella's evidence. If *Rough Justice* had not made that tape recording, Josephine would have been called to give evidence, she would in all probability have stuck to her story and our appeal would have been rejected.

On Thursday 21st February 1994 Alan Goldsack and I took the train to London to present our case in the Court of Appeal. It had been hard work. After starting out with nothing but belief in the case, we had secured a legal aid order to carry out certain investigative work. When that was completed we made a further application for Counsel to advise as to the appeal and once the grounds of appeal were settled, we had been granted a further legal aid certificate to cover the hearing.

The events of the next day would prove if it had all been worthwhile. Alan had an open mind about the outcome but I was convinced that all would be well.

When we arrived in London our first job was to deliver Alan's skeleton argument to the court office at the Court of Appeal. A skeleton argument is a document prepared out of courtesy for the court. It sets out in brief how the defence intend to proceed and what submissions it will make to the court in relation to the case. It gives the judges some idea of what the case is about and can help to save time.

On finding the Royal Courts, Alan went to the barristers' room to leave his robes and papers and I set off for the court office. The Royal Courts are truly marvellous and have an aura about them which makes me proud to be part of a great profession. As I walked down long echoing corridors I imagined brushing shoulders with some of the great personalities of the legal profession. I also found myself wondering how the world famous British justice system will survive when it is being forced into economies which can only harm real justice. How can we stop the dreadful stereotyping that is taking over? I remember the time when it was an event to go and see your solicitor. As an office junior I saw clients in waiting rooms wearing their Sunday best and smelling of mothballs. I remembered thinking that I must be getting old.

By the time I found the court office and delivered the papers I was hot and sweaty. I was wearing a heavy top coat and carrying my work case and an overnight bag. I headed for the hotel in Drury Lane for a shower and a change of clothes.

At 6 pm I had arranged to meet Stella, who had travelled down to London with a friend. I had booked her into the Baltimore Hotel because of its proximity to the Royal Courts which would prevent any problems with public transport the following morning. After washing and changing my clothes I asked the hall porter directions to the Baltimore Hotel. He explained the route telling me it was a fifteen minute walk. Twenty minutes later I was lost. Spotting a well dressed chap with a leather briefcase I asked him for directions. He explained he was on his first trip to London from Poland but remembered passing the Baltimore only the day before. He gave me detailed but wrong directions and I ended up outside a massage parlour being stared at by a large evening-suited bouncer who offered me a VIP ticket and a good time. I told him that he was not my type and promptly walked off. I realized that the only way I was going to get to the hotel was to call a taxi. I hailed one and it stopped. Climbing in I asked for the Baltimore Hotel. The taxi moved less than fifteen yards down the road and stopped. The driver turned to me smiling and said "The Baltimore Hotel Sir". He refused payment but accepted the price of a pint for the entertainment.

Stella was waiting for me and told me that she had never stayed in an hotel like it before and was greatly enjoying the experience. We found a convenient place to talk in a little bar in the hotel itself where we proceeded to get down to business. Alan had prepared a number of questions which he wanted me to put to Stella and so I worked through them.

I also went through Stella's evidence again, but I was quite satisfied with her performance and took the view that she would be very reliable in the witness box. I should add, that giving evidence in any court is a difficult thing and the more serious the charge and the more important the court, the bigger the pressure. There was a degree of naïveté about the way Stella told her story and I felt this might stand her in good stead when she was cross-examined. I tried to prepare her as best I could without causing her too much alarm. I often find that witnesses can be put off by well-intentioned lawyers who go over the top in their warnings about what to expect. Stella was apprehensive, but she was not frightened because, as she explained, she could only say what she actually saw. It is often said in our profession that it is very difficult to trip up a truthful witness.

I joked with Stella that she must not drink too much because she would need a clear head for the morning and I believe that I left her feeling confident.

I managed to find my way back to Drury Lane arriving some time after 8 pm. I called at Alan's room where he was busily going through the paperwork for the umpteenth time. We had agreed to dine out that evening and we enjoyed a fine Italian meal spending the whole time discussing the case.

We walked back to the hotel retiring early because I had promised to see Stella again at 8 am the following morning. I had a leisurely bath in the hope it would help me to relax, but unfortunately sleep eluded me and so I spent some time writing a very long letter to my former employer George Tierney.

George was on one of his walkabout holidays and had travelled to South America to walk around Columbia and Peru. I think he set himself a target to see if he could spend three months there without being shot. His son Julian, who works at my office, had given me a postal address care of a post office in an obscure town in Columbia. I thought the letter might cheer him up and posted it the following morning only to find out two months' later on his return to England that he had never received it. I suppose it is still doing the rounds to this day.

I reflected a little upon my training and without doubt Crehan Tierney Harthill, as the company then was, was perhaps the best possible grounding one could get in dealing with criminal law cases.

Eventually I must have dozed off to sleep, but was awake again at 5.30 am preparing for the day ahead.

I met Alan for breakfast and despite having considerable pre-appeal nerves I managed to eat a hearty breakfast, including an extra sausage from an elderly waitress who I said reminded me of Marlene Dietrich. I set to find the Baltimore Hotel, this time with ease, and within five minutes Stella was downstairs. She had put on her best dress for the event telling me she thought wearing her leathers would not be a good idea. I agreed and we set off on the short walk to the Royal Courts.

We arrived early so that I could show Stella where she would give her evidence and to familiarize her with the room. This is often helpful to witnesses who can then concentrate on the business in hand rather than looking round the room taking in their surroundings.

We were greeted by Mark Calvert of the BBC and a camera crew. I gave a brief interview, taking great care as to what I said, bearing in mind that evidence was to be given that morning.

Other supporters arrived and I took them all into the coffee lounge which was on the ground floor. Shaun and Sharon (John's step-mother) had not yet arrived and so I left someone at the door to look out for them, while I went off to meet Alan near the robing room and from there the two of us went to the cell area where John was waiting to see us. John,dressed in black prison issue top and trousers with a dark denim jacket appeared to be quite nervous. This surprised me because throughout all my previous visits he had been extremely calm. He said very little but listened attentively as Alan went through the procedure of the court and explaincd what wc hoped would happen.

John had been given a change of clothes by one of his supporters but on inspection we thought his prison clothes would give a better impression. The prison staff were extremely pleasant and most helpful to us but I have to confess to feeling the odd butterfly sensation as I left to go up to the court.

It was 9.45 am, the Court was due to start within fifteen minutes, and Shaun had not arrived. Our entourage were all seated outside court number seven where our appeal was to be heard when Charles Hunter and one of his colleagues from *Rough Justice* arrived enabling us to hold a brief discussion about the matters in hand before I advised our group to take their seats.

I had one last look around for Shaun and Sharon and I spotted them at 9.55 am crossing the road in front of the court They had difficulties with the Tube but there was little time to discuss this as I took them straight into the court getting them into the public gallery just before Lord Justice Glidewell and his two colleagues made their entrance.

The atmosphere in the Court of Appeal is different from the Crown Court, and certainly from the Magistrates' Court . Court number seven is a large courtroom in the traditional style with old oak benches for the solicitors and barristers. Tradition and protocol are fiercely protected within this building where the lawyers' front bench is for the Q.C.'s and the middle bench for junior barristers which on this occasion was empty because we had been refused one by the Legal Aid Board. I had to sit a further row away which made communications between Alan and myself difficult. Lord Justice Glidewell was the chairperson of the three judges and he greeted both Counsel and briefly announced the procedure he would favour. Alan then began to address the court with his submissions in relation to the quest for leave to call fresh evidence.

Our argument in brief, was as follows:-

1. We accepted John Megson was properly convicted on the evidence heard by the jury at trial.
2. The jury heard no evidence from any eyewitness who was in a position to identify the participants. No

one was available to be called on behalf of the appellant (the appellant was John Megson) and all members of the Druids' group had given statements to the police claiming to have been asleep and seen nothing. It was always the Prosecution case that most of them were lying and that several were/must have been criminally involved in the accident involving the death of Stephen Rowley.

3. One member of the Druids' group was Stella Harris. She had come forward and given a further statement. In it she:-

   a. described the appellant being so drunk he had difficulty walking.
   b. had seen the appellant being knocked to the floor by the deceased before any violence was used on the deceased.
   c. had seen the appellant barely conscious on the ground while the deceased was being assaulted and killed.
   d. named the actual killer.

4. Stella Harris explained why she told lies initially and why she was not prepared to tell what she now says is the truth at the time of the trial. Her reasons related principally to her entirely understandable fear of the alleged actual killer and other members of the group who by implications were, at the very least, criminally involved in a very serious assault. Her explanation was plausible.

5. Accordingly, there was a reasonable explanation for the failure to give this evidence at the trial and it appeared that it would be likely to be credible.

6. If heard and not rejected by the Jury her evidence:

a. gave the appellant a defence to any allegation that he was the actual killer

b. in so far as the prosecution put their case alternatively on a joint enterprise basis it:

[i] raised the question of whether, by reason of his drunken state, the appellant had, or was capable of forming the necessary intent for murder.

[ii] raised the question of whether the appellant knew a weapon was to be used and whether the necessary intent for murder should be inferred.

c. was capable of giving the appellant a complete defence to both murder and manslaughter.

7. In the circumstances, the Court should hear the evidence of Stella Harris and, if of the opinion that a jury might believe her evidence, quash the conviction and order a re-trial.

8. There were no practical difficulties in the way of a retrial. Most if not all of the Prosecution evidence called at the original trial was admitted.

The reasons why Stella was credible were:-

a. The Prosecution themselves say that her (and others) original statements are untrue.

b. The reasons/motives for lying are obvious – initial group decision and then fear of dire personal consequences which were confirmed by approach after it is known she intends to *break ranks*

c. No great surprise her evidence stands alone because:

[i] A few really were asleep.

[ii] Several were involved and by telling the truth would incriminate themselves in serious crime.

[iii] Jo is still frightened and/or had been got at and/or just does not want to be involved and/or really did not see much.

d. What motive did she have for lying?

[i] She was never a particular friend of Megson.

[ii] She could have come forward earlier but thought that the men would stand up and be counted – and it would be better for Megson if they came forward.

[iii] Why should she name Jo as being present unless she was as this would only make complications.

She says some things which are not entirely helpful e.g., there was an earlier reference by Animal of stabbing, going for a *knock* without making it clear that Megson was not party to it.

Publicity seeking? – the BBC was not involved until long after she was.

e. What indications say that she is telling the truth?

[i] Explains injury to John Megson's mouth

[ii] Explains the presence of the deceased's blood on John Megson's clothing

[iii] Her version as to numbers agrees with Drakesmith/Richardson's accounts of the incident.

[iv] She names names – putting erstwhile friends/-colleagues at risk of substantial prison sentence (there was at least a 50/50 chance that the police would seize her statement and use the information which was just what they had been hoping for back in 1989)

[v] The whole story made sense.

It was clear from some of the comments made and questions asked by the judge that the court had considered the papers and considered them thoroughly.

My father used to use an expression *good manners cost you nothing* and this expression must have been known to Lord Justice Glidewell. His courtroom manner was a lesson to us all.

I deplore bad manners from people in authority especially when they use their rank to justify it. Magistrates and judges who behave badly ought to take time off to watch professionals like this. I think they would learn a lot for it is not a weakness to be well mannered, it is a strength. The idea that judges are entitled to be rude to everyone else because of their position puts them in a bad light.

My father was right. He usually was but unfortunately I didn't realize it until he was gone.

Mr. Bethel Q.C. for the prosecution raised no specific objection to the application respectfully leaving the matter to the court to decide as to whether they felt leave to call fresh evidence was appropriate.

The court considered the matter briefly and Alan was addressed by Lord Justice Glidewell who indicated that the court were granting such leave to call fresh evidence and invited him to call our witness. Owing to matters of procedure, Stella had been outside during the application which was normal for a witness who is likely to give evidence.

Stella was called in to the witness box and as the judges scrutinized her, it seemed to me they were trying to make an assessment of her demeanour as she arrived. I could positively feel the tension in the atmosphere.

At first Stella gave her evidence in a very quiet voice and in a most subdued manner and as Alan asked her his initial questions she appeared to be extremely nervous.

I remember that during her early evidence, she looked across at me, I smiled and nodded reassuringly although I felt I was in the witness box with her, such was the tension. Stella gained confidence with every answer and when Mr. Bethel began to cross-examine her, she was ready.

Martin Bethel Q.C. tried his very best to discredit Stella's evidence in his cross-examination, but she was quite determined and throughout she retained her composure. I kept an eye on all three Judges as they watched and listened intently to Stella's answers. There was never really an occasion when I thought she was going to be in difficulty apart from when Mr. Bethel cross-examined her about the television programme.

He tried to suggest that her evidence was not completely consistent with the script and I panicked.

My immediate reaction was that the prosecution had found a chink in the armour and I must confess my heart sank. In the agony of the moment I thought I saw our case begin to fall about our ears. However, Stella innocently and directly announced:

"But I didn't make the programme."

I breathed a sigh of relief. What a brilliant answer it was, and so simple.

Mr. Bethel completed his questions and it was then the turn of the three appeal judges to ask more questions which further prolonged the ordeal, but I really believed that they were with us. Stella had been in the witness box for an hour which was probably the longest hour of her life. To me it felt as long as my career to date.

As she left the witness box and walked past me she whispered, "Did I do all right?"

"Brilliant." I whispered in reply and she took a seat behind me. I looked across at Charles Hunter who gave me the thumbs up sign, obviously thinking we had done enough. All through the proceedings John sat passively and listened with his head slightly bowed. Alan turned round to face me. Although his face was expressionless, he raised his eyebrows as if to ask "Well?"

Mr. Justice Glidewell invited Alan to sum up his case after which the bench announced that they would retire to consider their evidence and return after lunch.

Outside the courtroom we all planned our movements over the lunch break. Charles and the *Rough Justice* team went off with Shaun, Sharon and the other supporters who of course included Stella. Alan and I went to the public house across the road where we spent the whole ninety minutes discussing the case, anticipating the possibles and the probables with arguments for and against. It was soon time to return to court and so we set off not really knowing what to expect.

It was cold outside but bright, and substantially different from the day before when we had left a snow-covered Yorkshire. On the way I noticed the television cameras ready to get some footage to add to their story for the evening news and Alan, not a man who likes publicity, dodged them as he moved quickly into the court while I let them get me trying to put my best side to the cameras. We were followed by Stella and the rest of the group. She tried to avoid the cameras but Shaun made no such attempt.

We were to laugh about it later.

The court room was soon filled with people and expectation. John was brought back into the dock and he looked towards his supporters and waved. Within a very short time, the judges entered the court, bowed in a measure of considerable majesty, and sat down. Lord Justice Glidewell began to speak.

My pulse was racing and my heart beating so much I could hear it.

I expected a rather long summing-up with the outcome saved until last but we were soon out of our misery. The

Lord Justice announced the appeal was allowed, the conviction quashed and he ordered a re-trial. Our supporters greeted the announcement with cheers but John just looked at the ceiling, drew a deep breath and looked across at us, his face blank. He was in a state of shock.

We waited in a tiny interview room and I couldn't help thinking what notorious criminals must have trod those well worn corridors, but I was distracted from those thoughts with John's arrival. He was still in a state of shock and really didn't know what to think. For nearly five years he had been without any real hope and now he was one step from freedom but dared not dream of the future. I told him I would visit him at the earliest opportunity. We set off to go and I recall that John uttered just the one word "Thankyou" as he was led away.

His reaction was odd because although he was obviously pleased he explained that he was frightened to build up his hopes in case they should be dashed at the last hurdle. I had passed on all his family's best wishes but our meeting had been very brief.

A re-trial after five years is relatively rare and has to take place within a strict time scale. It was set to begin on 20th May 1994 and John Megson would remain in custody until his re-trial.

The order of a re-trial was a considerable achievement but the reality was that we had put John back into the same position he was in prior to his first trial. In short, he was still charged with a murder which he was going to have to stand trial for and so he was remanded in custody pending the trial. It was a tremendous relief but all we had earned was the right to have a new trial. He was still far from being found not guilty.

John could still be convicted of murder and this was an important consideration.

We had discussed with John the possibilities and the main concern was the re-trial itself. What would we do if he was convicted? It was a dreadful situation but it had to be faced.

One possibility was to offer a guilty plea to manslaughter. After all, John had already served five years and he was not going to get that time back so his release might then have been assured. He was certainly present when the fight took place and his presence there was indicative of someone who was prepared to be involved in disorder. Subject to the basis upon which a guilty plea could be tendered, John was prepared to admit manslaughter. Alan canvassed the point with Martin Bethel Q.C. but the prosecution made it quite clear that it was murder and nothing else. As a result we were resolved to fight a trial.

When we got upstairs we were greeted by Shaun and the rest of the group with the television cameras waiting outside. Alan went to the robing room to change while I faced the cameras and the press on the steps of the Court building.

Within minutes, Alan had joined us to walk across the road to the pub where I was greeted by Charles with a double gin and tonic in one hand and a glass of Champagne in the other. I turned to find Alan with a glass of Champagne in *both* hands. "Typical," I thought and promptly drank the gin to concentrate on the good stuff. We were all elated but unfortunately, we couldn't stay for the party and after a while we set off for Kings Cross and home. We were soon in a taxi and on the train.

We got a seat with a table where Alan promptly went

to sleep. I spent the next hour on the mobile phone after Kate had rung with a list of call backs which I dealt with as best I could.

One of the calls was to BBC Radio Sheffield and the Winton Cooper Show. Unfortunately, the carriage was rather noisy so I beat a hasty retreat to the lavatory which seemed to be quieter as if it was not in use. The BBC rang me back and Winton asked me where I was speaking from so I told him that I was in the Kings Cross to Doncaster bog and he replied to the effect that the interview was going out live! I had put my foot in it again and at the end of the interview, I finished by saying, "This is Steve Smith for BBC Radio Sheffield in a bog on a train."

I returned to my seat to see Alan sleeping soundly but I was still too keyed up to relax so I went to the refreshment bar where I found Mark Calvert and the BBC team boozing away merrily. I joined them for a while before returning to my seat with a gin for Alan to find him still asleep. Not wanting to waste his ice, I drank the gin and tonic and pinched his phone because my battery had run out.

Within two hours we were back in Doncaster having arranged transport from the station and within another hour I was home. I couldn't understand why I wasn't tired but I was to find out the next day when the exhaustion finally caught up with me. The adrenalin factor had overridden my tiredness during the previous week so I turned on the late TV news and cringed as my interview came on. I was not impressed but it didn't seem to matter.

I have to confess I had a wonderful time and how I wished that all my working life could be like that. The next day I had off but I felt guilty being idle and thought

I ought to have been working. I was pondering such thoughts when the telephone rang. It was Shaun Megson.

Shaun told me that he caught the late train back from London and had been up all night re-living the events of the day.

I told him we must keep our feet on the ground and must not get carried away since this was only the start of it. What really counted was the re-trial for which this had been a mere preview with the main part yet to come. "We'll do it!" said Shaun enthusiastically.

"I hope so Shaun," I said, "I really do."

We had come so far but now we had a lot of work to do and on the Monday morning I started again.

XII

Preparation for the Re-Trial

> Or have I dream'd the bearing of our knights
> Tells of a manhood ever less and lower?
>
> *Tennyson*, Idylls of the King

Although much work had been done for the appeal we had been operating on a restricted legal aid certificate and it was only after a full certificate to include Junior Counsel was granted by the Court of Appeal, that we were able to set about doing much of the work that was required.

A re-trial is a new hearing before a fresh judge and jury and obviously the case would be put in a different way, certainly from the point of view of the defence, because this time the full story would come out as Stella would be giving evidence again.

It was necessary to visit John fairly regularly to go through the statements in great detail. Any prospective witnesses had to be interviewed and statements taken. Worst of all was the consideration and noting of the tapes of interviews with the Druids in Scarborough. In 1989 the police had just started conducting interviews on tape and now almost all interviews between the police and suspects are conducted in this way. It has been suggested that interviews should be conducted on video so that juries would be able to note the defendant's reactions to questions. If the money can be found to fund this idea, my belief is that the conviction rate will go up as so many defendants look so guilty when interviewed.

The idea to consider the tapes of the interview came from Alan Goldsack in one of our many meetings on the matter.

The tapes had not been considered before and little did we know how important they were to be in our defence. I asked the prosecution to supply us with tapes of interview of all the people questioned. Following my request I received a telephone call from Inspector Morris of the prosecutions department of Scarborough police. He was most helpful but I was put on my guard when he asked me if I was serious. Why would he ask that? I soon found out when he told me that the tapes ran for up to forty-five minutes each and there were ninety of them!!

Thank you Inspector Morris, I thought, and thank you, Mr. Goldsack!

It was obvious the tapes had not been heard before because copies had to be made and as there were so many, arrangements were made for me to collect them from Leeds Crown Court when we attended the pre-trial interview. On receipt, I telephoned Alan to tell him how many tapes I had received. He wished me well!

Although it would not have been John's first choice of prison, Armley was handy for me because whenever I needed to see him I was able to use a friend and fellow solicitor's office as a lunchtime base and somewhere I could get some work done. Bernard Ewart had been a prosecutor with the Crown Prosecution Service before setting up his own solicitor's office in Armley. In the build up to the re-trial I was to become a regular visitor and many a lunchtime Bernard would introduce me to his many local public houses. Bernard is the perfect host and I well remember being invited to one of his weddings.

It was a spectacular affair which began at Leeds Registry Office. After the ceremony, all the guests were taken by coach to a day at York Races. On the journey we were treated to Champagne and smoked salmon with Bernard weaving up and down the gangway keeping the glasses filled. When we arrived the sun was shining and the crowds looked marvellous. The ladies were resplendent in their beautiful dresses and many of the men were either in traditional racing dress or wearing striped blazers and straw boaters. It had the effect of a trip back in time. The scene was one of gaiety and laughter and Bernard treated his guests to his special guided tour of the racecourse. The first part of the tour was to a drinks tent. From there we were led to a Champagne tent and then on to a Pimms tent. As the tour progressed I became less aware of where we were being taken but I recall arriving at the show ring where the horses parade before taking part in the races. At this point one of our party, an elderly Irish woman who had come over just for the wedding, was heard to say,

"Well, they have everything here. They've even got their own dog track."

We were all convulsed with laughter and it didn't matter if it was her comment or the Champagne and Pimms which caused it. We had a wonderful day and although I'm not a gambler I placed bets on all seven races. The races commenced at two thirty and in the first event, my horse fell at the first fence. In the second my choice fell at the second fence and the third it was scratched. In the fourth race the horse didn't run because the jockey had gastroenteritis and I wouldn't be surprised if the horse had nits. In the next race I had backed an Irish combination which didn't turn up. In the penultimate race my horse didn't finish but the best was saved until the last when the jockey got caught under the starting gate and was trampled on by the other riders.

Fortunately, he was not hurt and managed to scramble free of the irate punters who were chasing him across the paddock. The day finished much as it had begun and on the journey home we were treated to a number of renditions from the well known works of Gilbert and Sullivan by an out of tune but well oiled Ewart.

I had been fitting my preparation work for the re-trial into my ordinary schedule but it was difficult. Saturday mornings were usually spent with John at Armley and after each meeting I prepared a file note showing what I had done and how long it had taken. I was acquiring a mass of paperwork and it all needed collating. Kate, my Secretary, had the burden of putting it all together and keeping it in order. We were also still receiving papers from the Crown Prosecution Service and this meant more preparation work. In addition to all this I had the tapes to listen to!

As the trial date approached, I was conscious that I was not making progress with the tapes as quickly as I wanted. I decided that I had to spend as much time working with them as possible and to help me tackle over sixty-five hours of taped interviews I bought a Walkman portable tape recorder which I played at every opportunity.

I used the car cassette player on my way to the office, on my way home and on every other car journey I made, but when I was going anywhere on foot, out came the Walkman.

What little spare time I have I like to spend in our large garden. I like the peace and quiet and love to listen to the birds sing and watch Charlie our Labrador dog chase, but never catch, members of the indigenous population of squirrels. The Walkman took away the peace and quiet but I found I could work in the garden and listen to the tapes at the same time, only breaking off to make notes of any interesting points in the interviews. I dictated these notes into my portable dictaphone which I carried around with me in a home made holster attached to my belt. With the Walkman clipped to one side, the dictaphone to the other and headphones over my ears my hands were free to use any garden tool as I listened.

I looked like Billy the Kid and I soon became quick on the draw. On hearing anything important relating to the case, my right hand would immediately drop to the holster bringing the weapon out and *cocking* the *record trigger* in a lightning sweep. I would discharge a trail of verbal *bullet* points and the weapon would be back in its holster in a blur of motion. I then returned to the gardening until the next time. It was a complicated procedure which looked peculiar but was most effective until my friend Newton Wright the local farmer brought me a ten ton load of cow manure. I was in the garden one Sunday spreading copious quantities of the revered mixture, when, as I bent down to move some of it round an Azalea bush, I caught the wire leading from the Walkman in my belt to the headphones. They shot off my head and landed in the middle of a pile of the well rotted manure.

As I tried to extract them the dictaphone fell into it as well. The next day the typist was horrified because the dictaphone switch had a hair trigger and the fall had managed to record my observations at the time for posterity. I must confess I was not well pleased but then neither was the typist, who was a confirmed Methodist.

The Walkman followed me everywhere I went, the garden, the toilet, the bath, the pub and even to my mate Chris Good's house on my Saturday visits for the bacon fry-up lunches. Last of all, I played them in bed and instead of sheep, I was counting Druids! Not all the recordings were clear and some had to be replayed which took even more time.

The content was interesting because it showed how difficult it was for the police to break down the Druids story in an attempt to get at the truth, as at each twist and turn, there was the *Code of Silence*. This worked well until I began getting *trigger* happy and started losing concentration. But then it happened.

There can be no doubt that it was worthwhile. It was not until I listened to the taped interviews with Animal (Colin McCombie) that I realised just how important the tapes were. In one I heard the police refer to the fact that John had been charged with murder. The officer told McCombie it would not be right for John to take the responsibility if he had not killed Rowley. I thought that was an interesting remark to make, and it led me to believe the police had suspicions elsewhere. Indeed, in one of McCombie's interviews it was actually put to him that he was responsible for the Rowley murder.

When I listened to Woodhead's taped interviews I heard the police putting to Woodhead that there had been meetings at the club house after the Druids were released. The police suggested that those meetings were used to consolidate the Druids' story. At first Woodhead denied that any such meetings had taken place, but the police told him they had carried out observations at the house and had seen them arrive. D.S. Bell even described the type of motorcycle Woodhead had arrived on and most importantly told him on tape that he was accompanied by Josephine on the pillion of the motorcycle and that she had accompanied him into the club house. No one could have known that the *throw away line* was to be so important later on.

I immediately realised that this conflicted with Josephine's statement to the police because she had told them in her later statement that she was not at any of the subsequent Druid meetings. It was *manna from heaven.* I could not only damage the credibility of Josephine's statement but destroy it, and my witness in support was a police officer!

I slept well that night secure in the knowledge that the hours spent listening to the taped interviews had proved invaluable.

Winston Churchill said there was no such thing as luck, but success was merely a question of good preparation. I am not sure I entirely agree with the great man, but what I have found over the years in this profession is that hard work and good preparation are never wasted. At times the product of much preparation is not needed to win a case but the day always comes when thorough preparation proves to be vital to the outcome.

John Megson's case was proof of this.

As I had been looking over the papers, I realized the prosecution would be attacking the credibility of our star witness Stella Harris. I was trying to think of ways we could enhance that credibility. One of the ways I could have done that would have been to persuade Josephine to come forward and tell the truth, but unfortunately she was not prepared to do so.

One afternoon in the spring of 1994, I was appearing as ever in Rotherham Magistrates' Court on behalf of a client, when a thought suddenly struck me. If I could obtain a report from a forensic scientist to support our version of events, this would enhance Stella's credibility in the re-trial.

I was thinking about this just prior to applying for an adjournment on a case. I must admit that the thought totally preoccupied me and as the case in hand was a mere adjournment, it did not require a great deal of consideration from the point of view of content. My colleague Jonathan Ford who was assisting me in the court that day, passed me the adjournment file and told me that the client wished to change his address. I noted that he was on bail to reside at 76 Dalton Grove. This is known as a condition of residence and means that if the court orders a defendant to reside at that address, he has to live and sleep there every night. This man wanted to live somewhere else. Unfortunately he had a speech impediment which meant that his words were unclear.

You have to think on your feet in court proceedings and you are sometimes given instructions in the well of the court by whispers and you have to act accordingly. This can sometimes give the impression that you are not well prepared, but unfortunately this is how things are and you have to put up with it. The other problem is that defendants sometimes forget to mention things until the last minute.

Jonathan had told me about the change of address, but because we were all under pressure and were thinking of other things at the time, the details of the new address escaped me. I made the application to the magistrates, saying that it was vital that he change his address from 76 Dalton Grove, and trying to look as casual as possible, I turned to my client and said, "And what is the new address please?".

My client replied quite firmly "75 Dalton Grove". I was stunned by the remark and looked to see if I could see Jonathan, but he had gone.

I couldn't think of anything sensible to say, and based on the teaching of my former mentor George Tierney, I smiled at the Bench, with the smile that says "Well I'm in the shit now," and I proudly repeated the new address.

Before my buttocks had reached the seat, the Chairman who was entering into the spirit of the occasion said, "But Mr. Smith, this appears to be next door?"

Rising to my feet, I could only think of two words to say but I desisted and said "Correct Sir," and I promptly sat down.

The Chairman was well up to the occasion and with a wide grin on his face asked me "Is there a reason why he wished to change his address please Mr. Smith?"

I hadn't a clue, but I didn't want to admit that I had not asked. So I said the first thing that came into my head "Well, Sir," and then after a short pause "I understand that it is a much better area!"

Again, to indicate I was not being cheeky, I had a

broad smile on my face. It was not the "Well I am in the shit now," smile, it was the "I'm trying to be a witty bugger smile," which I prefer. Fortunately, this was a Chairman with whom you could enjoy a rapport and everyone enjoyed the joke before we got back to the serious business of the case.

It is always so much easier to appear in front of magistrates who are prepared to show a human face, and providing you do not go over the top, you can sometimes bring amusement into the proceedings at an appropriate point.

As we left the court I asked the client why he wanted to change his address; I couldn't help but smile when he told me, "It's a much nicer area!"

During a break in the proceedings, we went to the canteen in the recently opened Rotherham Court House. No more were we to suffer the litter strewn corridors or smoke stained ceilings of the old building. The new building is a non-smoking zone, a fact we are reminded of at least twenty times a day by way of the infernal tannoy system. There are facilities such as toilets, interview rooms, advocates' rooms and above all a very pleasant canteen which prepares bacon sandwiches in the mornings.

It is a popular area where the lawyers sit and discuss their cases and make the various agreements as to evidence, witnesses and the like. It is also the area where you pick up information about the day's events, the joke of the day or the most amusing case.

An incident can occur in one of the courts and within seconds the information is transmitted to the tea room and beyond.

As I was eating my bacon sandwich, my thoughts

returned to the Megson case and in particular the question of the forensic evidence. I decided to telephone Alan Goldsack that afternoon and bother him yet again with one of my ideas. We arranged a case conference, and when I arrived I became aware that Alan had his own ideas about the forensic evidence.

After a discussion, we decided that I would instruct a forensic scientist to carry out certain tests for us. We were to give him full details of the prosecution case and let him have sight of Stella's statement, the medical and pathologist's evidence, and ask him to consider it. We then wanted to gain access to the old exhibits in the case if they still existed and in particular John Megson's clothing. We wanted the scientist to compare all this information and the blood staining on the clothing, and see from that whether Stella's version of events was acceptable in forensic terms. If this was agreed, we would have forensic evidence to support Stella's version of events.

The difficulty with this approach was that the forensic scientist could have reported that his tests on the clothing showed that the fatal blow could not have been delivered in the way that Stella had described. I had to consider this course very carefully indeed. If we wanted to gain access to the original exhibits, we would have to approach the prosecution for their consent to do so, and if we were sending a forensic scientist to inspect them, the prosecution would be unlikely to allow us to do that unless they had their own expert present as well.

This represented a considerable risk, for clearly the prosecution would be privy to our findings. I was rather surprised that they had not thought about this themselves, but I suppose it may have also been a risk for them.

I decided to visit John and explain what I had proposed to do. He agreed with everything that I had said, and reiterated that he would leave everything to me and that I should proceed with the case in whatever way I thought fit.

I explained to him the dangers of this course of action and he replied that it was only a problem if the incident had not occurred in the way that Stella had described. John had complete faith in Stella's account of what had really happened.

The main difficulty that we had, was in relation to the exhibits. Fortunately they had been kept and so I prepared all the papers for the scientist sending them to him without delay, as I was very aware that we were running out of time.

All I could do was to sit and wait for the forensic evidence, which was to prove to be more dramatic than I thought possible.

Everything seemed to be coming together at the right time, but it is a mistake to be too confident in this profession. A case can look a winner on paper, but can then fall to pieces when your client gives evidence. I cannot count the times that I have done well by attacking the credibility of prosecution witnesses, to be let down by aggressive or foolish clients when giving their own evidence.

I remember one such case when the prosecution witnesses were poor and my client remarked that we were onto a winner. I told him that he must give evidence, and that he must keep his cool and not lose his temper, but unfortunately he failed miserably. He was a dreadful witness, arguing with everybody including the prosecutor, the clerk of the court and the magistrates as well. When the magistrates convicted him, he blamed me.

XIII

The Re-Trial

> Pray let no quibbles of lawyers, no refinements of Casuists, break into the plain notions of right and wrong, which every man's right reason and plain common-sense suggests to him. To do as you would be done by, is the plain, sure and undisputed rule of morality and justice. Stick to that.
>
> *Lord Chesterfield*

One thing that never ceases to surprise me is the twists and turns the law can take. Despite all the preparation and all the planning things can alter in a minute, dramatically affecting the outcome of a case. As we began the build up to the final hearing, there were a thousand and one things to do. By the final week our forensic evidence still had not arrived. The Home Office forensic expert had been unavailable, resulting in our expert being unable to inspect the items of clothing. I made call after call trying to set the inspection up. I thought everything was conspiring against me. In the middle of all this I was shocked to be informed by Alan that there was a problem about the hearing date. It was the Wednesday before the trial was due to start on the Monday 20th May, 1994, that he contacted me to say that Mr. Justice Holland would no longer be dealing with the case and the appointed trial judge would now be Mr. Justice McFerson of Clunny.

Mr. Justice McFerson had been dealing with the case of Robert Black who was infamous as a child murderer and this trial was to finish on the Thursday afternoon, leaving the judge free on the Friday.

The suggestion was that John's case was actually a six-day case, and therefore it would be brought forward to the Friday. I rather suspect that the reason for this was that the court did not wish to leave the High Court judge without work for the day, and so John's case was brought forward to suit his arrangements. Obviously this caused a great deal of disquiet, not only with us but also in the prosecution camp. I have found in my experience that the best laid plans of mice and men are often changed by a High Court judge.

Thankfully, we were assured of our Counsel because our Junior Counsel Paul Watson was available, and Alan Goldsack was sitting as a recorder in Newcastle and he could simply cancel his Friday sitting. My arrangements were relatively inconsequential although I had planned to take the day off to tie up any loose ends in the case.

The prosecution, however, were grievously affected because their Leading Counsel Martin Bethel Q.C. was unavailable for the Friday. From what I gather from my opposite number at the Crown Prosecution Service they had been told to *lump it*. Perhaps understandably they were extremely upset about this development and decided to object to the case being brought forward.

There were a number of telephone calls with the result

that the prosecution were allowed to mention the matter before one of the judges at Teeside, with a view to seeing if there was any merit in their application to adjourn the case.

If the judge considered there was any merit in the prosecution application, the matter would be listed the following day which was the Thursday, to allow the defence to make representations. This did not happen, because the prosecution were merely told that the case would go in on the Friday, and they would have to instruct new Leading Counsel.

I had a great deal of sympathy for the prosecution on this point because Mr. Bethel had not only conducted the original trial, but also the case in the Court of Appeal when Stella Harris gave her evidence and it seemed logical that the same counsel should continue to act.

I am bound to say that if this had happened to the defence at that late stage, there would have been all manner of applications and I rather suspect that no court would have ordered a change of defence counsel so late in the day.

At the Court of Appeal in London, Martin Bethel had made it quite plain that the charge of murder would stand and there would be no room for negotiations as far as a plea of manslaughter was concerned. However, we believed that a fresh mind on the case might bring forward a different view.

Leading Counsel Mr. Guy Whitburn Q.C. was instructed for the prosecution. There can be no doubt he must have worked incredibly hard over the course of the next day or so to be able to grasp the salient points in the case. He was, of course, assisted by Mr. Andrew Robertson as Junior Counsel who had been with the matter throughout. I felt that Mr. Whitburn may have had a different view from Martin Bethel and I was soon proved to be right. Alan had telephone consultations with Mr. Whitburn as normally happens in cases of this sort, and told him that if a charge of manslaughter was to be considered, then the defence would certainly give consideration to it. Mr. Whitburn was not aware that manslaughter had been talked about as long ago as the Court of Appeal.

On Thursday, I had a full court list and quite frankly I could have done without it but one of the cases I was dealing with was extremely interesting although compared with the seriousness of the Megson case, it paled into insignificance.

It was about a man who was taking his horse for a walk late one night when he claimed that the police seized him, beat him up and arrested him alleging that he had stolen the horse. When he was found to be the owner, the police promptly charged him with being drunk in charge of a horse.

The case had attracted a deal of media attention and a representative from Yorkshire Television was present at the hearing and requested an interview. I had a fairly busy list but managed to find time to do the interview and the list as well. We discussed whether a man should be free to take his horse for a walk at midnight and the case provided a great deal of amusement. Later that day when I returned from the afternoon session I received a fax of a statement prepared by the prosecution from their forensic scientist.

Our forensic specialist had conducted the various tests on the clothing that we had asked for and in conjunction with the prosecution specialists had prepared a report upon which both parties were agreed. Obviously in a case like this, prospective professional witnesses like to discuss cases with their counterparts if at all possible. It is sensible for the forensic evidence to be agreed but this is not always the case. The forensic statements arrived shortly before our own expert's report and they were substantially in agreement.

The conclusions reached by both experts were vital to the case and were as follows:

Summary of Bloodstain Distribution on John Megson's Clothing

LEATHER JACKET – There was heavy bloodstaining on the lower left sleeve in and around the zip, on the inside of the cuff and on the upper left sleeve. Smears of blood were also present on each lapel and some of the blood from the left lapel could well have originated from Megson himself, but not from Rowley.

DENIM JACKET – There were small light smears of blood mainly on the upper left front.

OUTER JUMPER – There were heavy spots of blood on the outside front and heavy bloodstaining on the left cuff with a smaller amount of blood on the right cuff.

INNER JUMPER – There was some bloodstaining on the left cuff and a little on the right cuff.

There was no bloodstaining on the jeans, left boot, or leather trousers. A single tiny spot of blood was present on the right boot.

The grouping results described in an earlier statement showed that the bloodstains on the left sleeve and left cuff of the leather jacket, and on the front and left cuff of the outer jumper could all have originated from ROWLEY but not from MEGSON (or indeed from any of the other individuals from whom blood samples were submitted).

COMMENTS – The pattern and the appearance of

bloodstaining on MEGSON's clothing indicates that MEGSON and ROWLEY have been in sustained (rather than brief or passing) contact while ROWLEY was bleeding. The bloodstaining could have arisen in a number of ways such as:

i) MEGSON stabbed ROWLEY, possibly holding him with his left arm and wielding the implement with his right arm.
ii) MEGSON held ROWLEY while ANOTHER individual carried out the stabbing, with MEGSON holding ROWLEY in much the same manner as (i) above.
iii) ROWLEY lay on top of MEGSON's left arm after he had been stabbed.
iv) ROWLEY was simply pushed away by MEGSON who used his left arm.

I am unable to determine which of the four alternatives is the more likely. In the appropriate circumstances, each could account for the bloodstaining on MEGSON's clothing.
2. Sara Gray added, Ms Harris also describes how a number of other men kicked ROWLEY's body to move him off the top of MEGSON. As ROWLEY was bleeding at this time I might have expected to find some blood on the footwear and/or on the lower trousers of one or two of the men unless of course none of the men came into contact with ROWLEY's upper body. There was, however, no bloodstaining which could be attributed to Stephen Lee ROWLEY found on the clothing of any of the other men allegedly involved in the incident.
3. The difficulty with these observations were that the police had not taken clothing from the other Druids and such clothing that was taken was taken a month later on

their arrests. Who was to say that they were the same clothes?

Clearly the key point was that Stella Harris' version was consistent with the forensic evidence and consequently the prosecution would not be able to exclude entirely that the possibility was true. I telephoned Alan with the news. We made no mention of manslaughter in that conversation but a conference was arranged and we decided that the full implication of the evidence could be discussed at that time.

I then received a fax from the shorthand writers firm who managed to trace the original tape from the trial in 1990 and we were given not only the transcript of the prosecutor's opening but also the transcript of the pathologist, Doctor Denmark's evidence. The transcript of the opening was important but Doctor Denmark's evidence was relatively inconsequential bearing in mind the turn of events in relation to the forensic evidence. I was trying to photocopy the reports but the office had closed and all the staff had gone home. I was making a fair effort when the machine ran out of paper. I eventually found a box but I didn't know how to take out the paper holder. I swore repeatedly at the machine and kicked it once telling it that I would throw it out into the rain which would turn it rusty. As I raised my foot to kick it a second time, I realized I was being watched in disbelief by our cleaner who had been busy opening a box of toilet rolls. "Bloody machine won't work," I said pathetically "can't get the paper in," I claimed attempting to justify my childishness. "Don't understand these Japanese models," I muttered.

With that, Madge picked up the paper, opened what appeared to be a secret compartment in the side of the copier and promptly reloaded the magazine with incredible ease. "I suppose you've done that before," I said seeking the assurance that I wasn't a complete idiot.

"No," said Madge "I just followed the instructions printed on the side of the machine." As Madge walked off with her sweeping brush in one hand and a box of toilet rolls in the other, I secretly questioned her parentage and completed my photocopying.

Before calling it a day, and heading for Teeside I had to call at Shaun Megson's house and deliver his rail tickets. As I walked to the car, my mind was already on the events of the following day and the important points of the case, hoping that I had everything under control. I was still trying to finish listening to the interview tapes when the unexpected sound of Animal (Colin McCombie) brought me back to the present. As I switched on the ignition, the interview with Colin McCombie blared out.

As I drove, I was busy listening to the tapes, dictating what I believed were important points into the dictaphone and answering calls on the mobile phone.

Somehow I got to the Megson household in one piece. I had warned Shaun the day before of the possibility of the trial being brought forward and we had agreed that it was pointless for them to attend on Friday because the court plan was that the jury would be sworn in, the prosecution Counsel would make his opening speech and any statements which were agreed would be read. Alan thought that we would probably be completed by lunchtime and the case adjourned for the live witnesses to be called on Monday. We believed that there was little point in dragging the Megson entourage up to Teeside for half a day. Shaun decided that they would travel up on the Sunday and indeed we had booked bed and breakfast accommodation for them at a farmhouse some fifteen minutes away from the Court. I gave him telephone numbers where he could get hold of me if required and I set off for Teeside with McCombie's gaelic utterances ringing in my ears.

By the time I got to Teeside I had finished listening to the last of the ninety tapes of interview.

I booked into the hotel and found a little fridge bar in my beautifully appointed room with a splendid selection of alcoholic beverages and half a carton of milk. I left the milk and concentrated on the Bacardi before having a leisurely bath. Taking the transcripts and the forensic reports with me, I then went down to a wonderful dinner and a bottle of my favourite red wine, Moulin à Vent. After dinner and a glass of Drambuie as a night-cap I set off for bed. I didn't sleep very well and was up early the next morning. After a very light breakfast I set off for the courthouse, arriving at 9.00 am. Alan and Paul Watson arrived at the same time and we went in to the court together. While they were robing I walked down to the cells to see John. He was remarkably calm and listened attentively as I updated him about the forensic evidence and what the implications were. I knew that this was as big a day for him as he would ever experience and I realised what a trauma it must be for him as he prepared to undergo a re-run of his trial of four years before.

With this in mind I did my best to make John feel at ease, offering him a cigarette which he was glad to accept.

By this time Alan had been able to see and discuss the forensic evidence with Mr. Whitburn. Both defence and prosecution were able to re-assess the case as a whole.

It now seemed clear that:

(1) The forensic evidence supported the defence case.

(2) Guy Whitburn became aware that the defence had always been prepared to plead guilty to manslaughter on an agreed basis.

(3) We were listening to the tapes of interview of the other suspects right up until the last moment. The information we received from the tapes provided material information. Not only had the original defence not heard the tapes but the prosecution had not either.

It wasn't until about half an hour later that Alan and Paul Watson appeared. Their continued absence had aroused my suspicions that something was happening and it came as no surprise to me when Alan asked me to step outside for a private word.

Alan reported that the prosecution had been talking about the possibilities of a plea to manslaughter. He asked me for my opinion which I gave readily saying that I thought it was entirely a matter for John to decide upon. However, before doing so I had to make sure on what basis such a plea could be tendered. The thing that meant most to John was that he should be cleared entirely of any suggestion that he had inflicted the wounds which led to Rowley's death.

My other two points were:

1. John did not go down to the Rowley encampment carrying any weapon.
2. He did not intend that anyone would be killed or caused grevious bodily harm.

Alan agreed with these propositions and we returned to John to explain what was going on.

I said earlier that you can never pre-plan cases like this but we could all sense that something important was going to happen and when I reported the position to John I could barely contain my excitement. I had not been given the *official nod* that this course would be acceptable but I thought it rather unlikely that we would be discussing it in this manner just for the hell of it. I asked Alan what he thought the sentence would be if this course was adopted. Alan believed that if John was sentenced to nine or ten years it would certainly be appealable, but there was also the prospect that the court might decide that he had actually served enough.

I decided to do the calculation to show what sentence would have to be imposed to bring about John's immediate release. We would then be in a better position to present our case to the Judge.

I asked the members of the prison service if they could check this for me. It resulted in a telephone call to the local prison for advice on the point. We discussed the issues with John and he indicated his desire to see a speedy end to the case and on the basis that he would be cleared of inflicting the wounds he would be prepared to plead guilty to manslaughter. I realized that such a plea would cause a great deal of confusion because the question that was bound to be asked would be how was it that John could plead guilty to such a charge after all that had been said in both the press and especially on the television programme. The answer to that is very straightforward. The prosecution opening, subject of course to our agreement would be on the basis that while John did not inflict the fatal wounds he was a member of a group that went to that scene and consequently he must have been aware that there would have been some form of illegal act and therefore he would be responsible, albeit to a lesser degree, for the consequences of that visit. There had always been the realization that the Druids were not paying a courtesy call but that some form of illegal activity was going to take place. Bearing in mind John's state at the time he would have had a relatively small responsibility in relation to the attack. John was satisfied with that and it was quite obvious that he did not wish to go through the trauma of a trial and giving evidence. Alan and Paul Watson decided to seek out the prosecution and see what final view they had come to. I decided to go with them so I could satisfy myself that we were doing the right thing. There were a number of consultations and I was finally told that the prosecution were prepared to accept a plea to manslaughter but more importantly were prepared to accept that plea on the basis that we had expressly outlined.

As I walked down to the cells to give John the news and let him make his decision, my mind wandered back to the television programme, wondering whether such an action would compromise anyone. Obviously it was John's case and his choice and it could not be influenced by anyone else's interest in the case. I recalled however the words of John Ware the presenter of the *Rough Justice* programme when he said ". . . but we don't believe that John Megson killed Stephen Rowley." I took the view that a plea on the basis of what we had agreed neither compromised John Megson himself or indeed those who had supported him particularly the *Rough Justice* team.

When I told John the news his face lit up with the clearest possible acceptance that I have seen in any defendant. Once again I went through the various formulae. Unfortunately the prosecution made it clear that if there was no plea to manslaughter there would be a trial, but the murder charge would stand. I felt that this was entirely reasonable on their part and was exactly how I would have dealt with the case were I acting for the prosecution. If he was to accept the plea to manslaughter he was likely to walk out of court that day a free man. If he chose not to accept he ran the risk, and indeed there had to be a risk, of being convicted of murder and having his life sentence re-affirmed.

I am convinced that anybody reading this and knowing the facts would make the same decision that John made. Even if he had run a trial and been completely acquitted, it still would have resulted in his release that day. To that extent he would not have improved his position because he certainly would not have been entitled to compensation for the five years he had served because he had largely brought the problem upon himself. It is true that John's record sheet would have been clear and the words manslaughter would not appear on his criminal record but balanced against the prospects of a life sentence it was too great a risk to take.

I have since considered the matter with a more open mind and while I think he would certainly have been acquitted of murder there was always the prospect that the jury might have found against us. How could I have possibly faced John and his family if I had influenced him to fight the whole case and we had lost. The responsibility was too great and I still think that he did the best thing.

The possibilities were three-fold:

1. He would be found guilty of murder.
2. He would be found not guilty of murder but guilty of manslaughter.

3. He would be found not guilty of murder and not guilty of manslaughter.

To deal with each point:

1. If he had been convicted of murder he would have been sentenced to life imprisonment and the judge could reconsider the recommendation that had previously been placed on the sentence and could have increased it if he thought it right. Obviously it would depend upon how the facts unfolded.
2. If he had been found guilty of manslaughter he would still have fought a trial and if the judge gained a particularly unfavourable impression, a substantial sentence could have been imposed.
3. A full acquittal was possible but unlikely in my view because at the end of the day the prosecution still had a young man who had lost his life and my experience of juries on these points is that the more serious the allegation the more likely the jury would be to convict. I thought that there would be enough evidence for a compromise verdict namely finding of manslaughter, so what would be the point of fighting a trial and losing any credit that we would get for pleading guilty.

I have since been asked what I would have done in those circumstances and this is a very difficult question for me to answer, but I suppose that if I had served five years on the basis that I had killed somebody when I had not and I had the prospect of bringing that sentence to an end I think it very likely that I would have adopted John's course.

I could not see how on the basis of our case a judge would impose a sentence of imprisonment in excess of seven and a half years. I chose that figure because I had worked out that if John was to be sentenced for no more than seven and a half years he would be released immediately.

Before we could go any further the judge had to be informed of the developments, for it was within his discretion to disagree with the course that was proposed. It was a matter therefore of common courtesy to speak with the judge in his chambers and inform him of the developments. In such circumstances solicitors are not privy to such chambers consultations. In years before it was not uncommon for Counsel to see the judge to obtain some form of indication as to the judge's views on the matter of sentence. This is a course which is now frowned upon, as courts prefer to deal with matters in open court. I think the old way was the best and most effective way of arriving at justice because at least the defendant knew exactly where he stood, as opposed to the lottery that it can now be.

Alan returned from the meeting with the judge to confirm his acceptance but also said that he had been given no indication at all of the possible length of the sentence, even though he felt very strongly that it was unlikely that the judge would impose a harsh sentence.

The indictment was put to John who pleaded not guilty to murder, but guilty to manslaughter. Owing to the swiftness with which this course of events had happened, I realized that the case would actually be finalized in the absence of John's family and friends. I made the point to him but he was anxious to resolve the matter and in many ways felt that it would be better if his family was not present. He was genuinely concerned about the pressures that they had been under during the five years of his incarceration, and whichever way the case went, the result would have to be momentous, and he could see that all the past five years frustrations would erupt either in a scene of elation or disappointment. We decided not to telephone Shaun to report what was happening and that we would wait until the actual result was known. The judge invited Mr. Whitburn to comment upon the plea that had been tendered for the benefit of the court and the public. To comply with the formalities of the court process he indicated to the judge that the plea had been considered by the prosecution on the basis of the new evidence which had only just been obtained. He emphasized this point because the courts are often very annoyed if cases which have been set for trial, end in a guilty plea. It means that an awful lot of work, time, and effort, has been wasted, and courts now believe that if any pleas are likely to be tendered, considered, and accepted, they should be done so at the pre-trial hearing, thus avoiding not only the time delay but the costs that are involved in preparing and arranging for a trial.

The judge indicated his consent and Mr. Whitburn addressed the court in the form of an opening of his case.

The judge interrupted on more than one occasion to say that he had read all the statements in the case, seen the photographs and seized all the salient points. At the end of Mr. Whitburn's address, the judge asked Alan a simple question. He asked what sentence would he have to impose to ensure John's immediate release? I had taken the opportunity of telling Alan that any sentence above seven and a half years would mean that he would not be released. However, I said that to cover for any matters of internal prison record the best thing to do would be to consider a seven year term which would remove any doubts at all about his release. Alan made that point to the judge and before he could make any address whatsoever the judge indicated that he was going to pass a sentence which resulted in his immediate release.

It was a considerable anti-climax for me after all the years of work and preparation that had gone into this case. Alan's plea in mitigation was not to be used, as the judge announced that he did not require his mitigation and promptly sentenced John to seven years imprisonment. It was not an anti-climax for John, it was a blessed relief. His release was assured. In passing, the judge was keen to comment that any injustice that there had been in this case was of John's own doing. He said that had these facts come out at the earlier trial, then it is likely that the case would have been dealt with much sooner. The judge didn't express a view as to what sentence would have been given but I rather suspect it would have been in the area of eighteen months to two years, out of which John would have served approximately twelve months. The judge was most keen, particularly in the light of the *Rough Justice* programme, to say that there had been no injustice caused by any fault or mistake of the court, and that he held John Megson totally responsible for what had happened. In my view the judge was probably right although I rather regretted his dismissive attitude. I know that judges are very keen to act in the public interest, and as we had gone through the prosecution opening, on the basis that justice had to be seen to be done, I would have thought at the very least the judge would have given consideration to what we had got to say. It was all too pre-ordained for my liking and this resulted in a substantial anti-climax.

When the judge made his announcement I looked across at John Megson and his face beamed with delight.

I gave the thumbs up sign to him and he winked back at me and he was then taken away from the dock. I went straight to the holding cell where John was delighted to see me. We were joined by Alan and Paul Watson and John thanked them as sincerely as he knew how.

I told him that I wished to speak to his father before the press got to him, because I knew that they would be wanting to record his views on the matter. I was extremely worried that they would get to him first, so I rang him but I was told that he had gone to buy a shirt for the hearing on Monday. I spoke to his daughter Donna and gave her the good news whereupon she immediately burst into tears. I told her that I would ring later. There was an amount of paperwork that John had to go through before his release, so I took up an invitation to lunch with Alan and Paul Watson at a local Cantonese restaurant. I returned to court at 2.45 pm to be greeted by the press and two sets of television cameras. I went to the cell area to find that John had been released and was sitting on his own waiting for me. It was one of those moments in a long career that you can always recall. He sat on a chair outside the cell area, with his head slightly bowed clutching a very large polythene bag containing all his worldly goods. When I arrived his face lit up and I said to him, "Your transport awaits, Mr Megson as does two television cameras and a boat load of press." He hadn't quite grasped the enormity of what had gone on and as we walked to the foyer area of the court we could see the press outside. Mark Calvert was representing the BBC. He saw us approaching and immediately instructed his cameramen to ready themselves.

What a scene it would have been for them, had Shaun and his family been present. That really would have been pure *showbiz.* As we walked to the door, John stopped and announced "I'm actually free!"

"Of course you are," I replied, realizing that what had happened that morning had just got through to him. I had not thought what would have been going through his head. After all, at 11.35 am he was serving life imprisonment but at 12.10 pm he was a free man. I'm afraid I do not have the ability to put into words how he must have felt and neither did he, because with the realization came the confusion. John had difficulty in answering the questions that were being put to him. I still think he was rather shell-shocked from what had gone on and indeed it had happened so quickly that neither of us had been able to gather our thoughts. He was asked questions about the other Druids and I felt it right to interrupt and refuse to answer such questions, because we were not aware whether or not the case was actually closed. There had been some talk of the case being re-opened and the former Druids being re-questioned, and so, I felt it right that we should keep a particularly low profile on these points. I remember John being asked what job he wanted, and couldn't resist making the answer for him when I suggested that he was considering becoming a prison officer. The interview went well and after a number of photographs had been taken, the press went away to present their story to the outside world.

John and I walked away to the car and John rocked with laughter at the sight of my tax disc holder with no tax disc in it. John joked that he didn't want to breach his prison licence by aiding and abetting a solicitor to drive without a tax disc. We both laughed and sped off to a hotel to treat John to his first pint of bitter in over five years. In the car we tuned to the local radio and listened intently to the news flashes concerning the case. On the way back to Rotherham we stopped off to phone his family. It was a wonderful experience to speak to Shaun and to hear him speak to his son. There could be no doubt in my mind that the meeting at the house would be something to savour and indeed I was not disappointed. When we arrived at Shaun's house there were a number of people outside awaiting our arrival. I heard someone shout, "He's here, he's here," and before we could get out of the car Shaun and his family appeared at the door.

As I got out, I watched father and son embrace and Shaun was in tears. It was a wonderful moment that I will always remember. I have to confess, I had a considerable lump in my throat. Shaun then spotted me and embraced me as well. I made the quip, "I didn't know you cared," but Shaun was too pleased to hear it. There were similar greetings from all the other members of the family and some of John's loyal supporters. I have never been so popular and I savoured every minute of it. We went into the house where I was treated to a half-pint glass of red wine because Shaun knew this was my favourite tipple. The BBC radio were waiting for us and a very polite young lady waited a long time for things to calm down before she asked for an interview. We gave an interview which went out live on the evening news programme. With the interview finished we returned to the house where a fantastic celebration began. John still appeared to be in a daze but retained his dignity at a time when I rather expected he might lose it. By that time it was 8.00 pm and I had previously arranged to be in Liverpool on a conference connected to another murder case. I hadn't expected that we would finish by the

Friday, and I had a number of calls to make to cancel arrangements, including accommodation for the following week. I left the Megson family with mixed feelings. It was going to be an incredible party but I rather thought that it should be a family affair and while I was more than welcome I thought it right to take my leave. I set off for Liverpool tired but at least ten years younger. I was already thinking how I could approach the Liverpool case because the Channel 4 television programme *Trial and Error* were very interested although they had not confirmed that they would actually make a programme. I couldn't help a feeling of *déjà vu*, although I realised that no matter how long my career was to last, I would never get another case quite like this. It had been the highlight of a very exciting career in which I had been allowed to build up a practice in my own way and run it as I thought fit.

I felt that I was rapidly reaching the stage of my career when I should stand aside for the younger people to take over the mainstream day to day court business. I yearned for the possibility of being able to pick and choose the cases I wanted. However the logistics of that and indeed the financial implications would not allow me to think about it further. Of one thing I was sure, and that was that I had absolutely no regrets about what had taken place, and the decision we had made in John's case.

XIV
The Wedding

> Marriage is a wonderful invention, but then again so is a bicycle repair kit.
>
> *Billy Conolly*

The case was over, the reviews in the press had ceased and people had stopped patting me on the back and asking after *the Biker.* Generally things were beginning to get back to normal: John had gone to Wales to see Stella, the BBC had pursued another project, and I was back at Rotherham Magistrates' Court doing the rounds.

I received a telephone call from John, to say that he was returning to Rotherham with Stella, to stay at his father's for a few days and he made arrangements to see me to discuss one or two problems that had arisen. He came to see me one Friday in July 1994. He appeared to be in good spirits, although he was disappointed in not being able to find a job. It had been two months since his release and the initial joy of freedom had begun to wear a little thin. He had become something of a cult figure amongst the biking fraternity, excluding of course the Druids whose own popularity was at its lowest level. John attended party after party, but he really wanted a job.

The level of attention he had was astonishing. Between the date of the first television programme and his release he had received hundreds of letters in support. Most offered him a home, and in some cases marriage. Some of the writers submitted photographs of themselves in a variety of naked poses, and the majority of them were women!

In mid July, I was attending Sheffield Magistrates' Court for one of our regulars who had ventured outside the Rotherham boundary when I received a call on my mobile telephone which had become a necessary part of my life. My messages were relayed to me including the news that Alan Goldsack had been appointed a Judge. It came as no real surprise as I had known him a long time, and from the very start of our business relationship I knew that was his destiny.

He was young to be a Judge, but had experience and ability in abundance. It was the end of a very successful career as a barrister and I knew that he would be missed by his chambers. I reflected upon the many cases that we worked on together over a twenty-five year period. I had given him one of his first briefs as a barrister, and certainly his first brief as a Q.C. I thought that winning the Megson case was a fine way to finish an illustrious career. I had enjoyed working with Alan and I would miss him but I realised that there was no stopping *Father Time* and for me it was the end of an era.

At the court, I bumped into an old pal of mine, a solicitor called John Thompson. I liked to listen to his advocacy when I was young and I was interested to see if he had changed his style. He hadn't. He was the same old boring fart I knew. I'm joking when I say that, because he is a gifted advocate with a strong, if not slightly weird, sense of humour.

"Good afternoon Thompson, how well you look even in that dreadful suit." I said pointedly. As children may read these chapters, I will refrain from repeating the reply he gave save to say he was wrong because my parents were married at both my conception, and birth.

I was given the latest news from Sheffield, and we both cursed the way the profession was going. I left him to go about his business, but not before he told me of his pending marriage.

"Poor bugger," I said ruefully. "You're dead right there," said Thompson, thinking that I was referring to him. I smiled in the knowledge that I was thinking of her, and bade my farewell. I completed my case and returned to Rotherham cursing the council on my way, for the stream of road works that blighted the town centre.

A little later I heard from Charles Hunter at the BBC. He told me that he wanted to film a follow up programme showing John and Stella after his release. When I told him that John and Stella were to be married, he was delighted. "What a way to finish the programme," he said enthusiastically. He wanted to do some extra filming as soon as possible and asked me to arrange for John, Stella and Shaun to be available at the end of July with a view to the programme going out in August.

I offered my garden for the filming which I thought the *Rough Justice* team would like. They were happy with the idea and we set a date in the hope that the weather would be good and everyone would turn up. I was very busy at the time with some serious cases, one of which related to another biker. I was visiting Armley Jail regularly to see a biker who had forty-two charges ranging from attempted murder, to blackmail. There were more statements than in the Megson case and it was extremely complicated. John's case had one main plot, this had twenty-five!

The news of the new programme gave me something to look forward to, and when Charles confirmed that they would come up on 31st July 1994, I couldn't wait for the day to come.

However, on the day they arrived I had an awful morning. I had a long list of cases, and three prisoners that I didn't know I had. I needed to be away at the very latest by 11.45 am because the crew were arriving at Noon.

One thing that is certain about criminal court work is that no matter how well you plan your day, some bastard has to come and spoil it. The bastard that day was Albert, who had been arrested that morning, for theft of a chemical toilet from the council. I was distraught. The Crown Prosecution Service didn't have their papers, Albert didn't have any cigarettes, I didn't have any time, and sixteen local authority road workers didn't have a port of call.

"I don't know what you wanted it for," I said to Albert, "The fact is that you have nicked it and you are on bail." "They won't lock me up for this," said Albert, "It's only a bog for Christ's sake," he continued.

"It's still an offence," I said.

"Not a serious offence," said Albert.

"Some poor sod might think it is," I complained.

"There was nobody in it when I took it," said Albert, with a wide grin.

"Oh, that's all right then," I said, dismissing the theft as just one of those things, having realised that I was speaking to a brick wall. "I don't think you will get bail Albert," I said regretfully.

"You can do it Mester Smith," said Albert, "Tha's been ont' tele."

I realised that Albert was on a different planet and no matter what I said he wasn't going to change his view. Of him it could truly be said that *there are none so blind as those who will not see.*

I was finished by noon and by then Albert had gone to that great *nick* [nick is slang for prison] in the sky called the Wolds. The court wouldn't accept his argument that it was only a minor offence and he was remanded in custody. I left the Court with the same haste that I entered it and set off for home.

It was a very hot day with the temperature in the eighties. The sky was clear and there was not a breath of wind. I arrived home to find that Charles and his assistant, Margaret Renton were already there. Charles is sometimes known as "Charlie" a fact which was to cause amusement just after his arrival. I have a yellow labrador and by coincidence, she is called "Charlie". She makes a habit of urinating on my lawn which creates brown patches wherever she does it. My mother, who lives in a flat which is attached to the house, is a *lawn person*; that is to say that she likes a nice green healthy lawn. She hates to see brown patches and when she sees the dog about to defile the grass, she shouts a vociferous complaint. As Charles was viewing the garden looking for suitable filming sites, he moved out of sight from my mother's window. My dog wandered into sight and just as she began to squat, my mother shouted a firm riposte.

"Charlie don't you dare wee on that lawn."

"I wasn't going to . . ." replied Charles the producer,

his words tailing off as he realised that the rebuke was not meant for him.

That's a marvellous start I thought to myself as Charles recounted the story on my arrival.

By 12.30 pm, everyone was there except John and Stella. For one awful minute we thought that they wouldn't appear. Charles was worried because of the time limits upon him and the cost of assembling the crew.

Eventually John and Stella arrived and everyone was relieved. The day went well and filming was completed by teatime. There were a number of interviews with John and I thought he performed really well. What impressed me most was a completely unsolicited comment about the deceased Stephen Rowley. It was the first time John had spoken in detail about him. He said:

> "It's hard to talk about because a nineteen year old lad died. It's good to be out but no matter how good it is for us, what's his family thinking? There's a geezer out there that has killed their son.
>
> Alright, they got somebody who was involved through being there but they still haven't got the geezer who's done it and no matter what happens now, nothing is going to bring their son back and that hurts a lot. It hurts that the person who's done it is not man enough to stand up and say "Yes I'm willing to do time for it."
>
> It hurts that I have been with these people for a lot of years and I trusted them with my life. We go out to a race meeting and then this happens . . .
>
> I'm just happy I'm nothing to do with these people any more, and that people know now that I'm not the one who stabbed him."

The last film to be taken was of John and Stella on the bike following a camera perched precariously at the back of a large van. David, the cameraman wanted a shot of John walking along the street. This was completed at the bottom of my drive. Shaun and I hid behind a wall when the shot was taken whistling *Colonel Bogey* as John walked past. It was the only time in three years that he had called his father and I a pair of bastards. We all had a good laugh and by 6.30 pm the cameras were packed away and the crew had gone. I was told that the programme was due to be shown on 25th August 1994 on BBC2. The initial programme would be used with the new filming edited as an update. The press showed a great deal of interest as did the magazine *Bella*, and the announcement of the forthcoming marriage had obviously increased the public interest in John and Stella.

The new programme, *Rough Justice: The Biker's Tale* was well publicized and gained good reviews but as it was broadcast on BBC2 at 11.15 pm it did not attract as large an audience as the first programme. However, everyone who saw it was pleased to tell me how much weight I had put on. Unfortunately for me, they were right and I vowed to go on a diet. By 3rd September, 1994 I had failed miserably but it was the day of the wedding and I set off for North Wales.

I arrived at the registry office with some time to spare and as I had never been to a biker's wedding, I didn't know what to expect.

The rain stopped just as I heard the distant roar of motorcycles. John was in the line as the motorcycles parked up on the registry office car park. The bikes were a considerable array of beautifully maintained pieces of machinery. They attracted a great deal of attention from onlookers who were fascinated by the different colours and styles of handlebars and attachments. The best was a custom built Harley Davidson which I valued at over £10,000. While the Harleys are not the fastest of the bikes available they are certainly the most prestigious and can best described as the Rolls Royce of motorcycles.

Stella then arrived separately in Elaine Jubb's car. She was wearing a black and purple dress with her favourite black boots. She told me that she had been out the night before on her *hen night*. She had consumed a great deal of drink with the result that she had got the virus that affects me from time to time. Her friends had brought her round by throwing her into the local duck pond. Her boots were still wet the next morning but I don't think the damp registered.

As the bikers arrived so did the press. Cameras were clicking and John seemed quite perturbed by the whole thing. As the television cameras were being set up, the party was ushered into the office. If you suffered from claustrophobia this was not the best place to be. About thirty people squeezed into the small office. Many of them were bikers of varying sizes, ranging from big, through very big to massive. The registrar was a demure lady and was clearly ill at ease.

After the ceremony, John was invited to kiss the bride.

"What for, they are married now," came the comment from one of the esteemed guests. The joke broke the silence and the group departed down two flights of stairs to the awaiting press. After the photographs the group began to disperse, leaving me with representatives of Harlech T.V. and various newspapers. After the interviews, I set off for the pub that was to host the wedding party.

I was unable to join in with the drinking because I had to drive back to Yorkshire, but I managed two pints in the company of John and his friends. They were most hospitable and I found their conversation most entertaining. It was soon time to leave, however, and after saying my farewells I walked back to the car ignoring the rain.

I aimed to be back home by 5 pm as I was the twenty-four hour duty solicitor, and had to be available to deal with any emergency at any time within that period. The difficult period is between 11 pm and 2 am, especially at weekends. Every cuckoo who gets locked up at the weekend wants a solicitor. The majority of them are after cigarettes as they try to work the system to their advantage. The drunks are the best as they try to convince you that they are not drunk at all and they don't have to give a breathalyser because they didn't do anything wrong. One told me he didn't have to blow because he had got a sick note. I requested him to read it out to me over the telephone. The note said *pain in foot*.

I thought he was in pain somewhere else as I explained a potted version of the breathalyser law, while trying to stay awake.

"You had better get your arse down here," he said. "And bring me some fags." I explained that I wasn't a tobacconist and my *arse* was staying where it was and as politely as I could, I put the phone down on him.

As I drove home I took a wrong turning and ended up in Flint! There is one place worse than Flint in the rain and that is Flint in the snow. One word of advice: if you have to go there, don't ask for directions from ageing joggers and avoid the Mussolini Museum.

I returned to the office on the Monday. By now the staff were used to seeing me on television and so little comment was made about the TV coverage of the wedding. It seemed that everyone was sick of hearing about it and I knew we all had to put the case behind us.

As I got to my room, Peter told me that his mother was not impressed when she saw me on television wearing a jumper at the wedding. She had commented that I usually looked so smart but that a jumper at a wedding was a definite "No, no!" She was most probably right but the wedding hadn't been a suit and tie *do* and I'm sure that I would have ended up in the duck pond if I had turned up looking like a solicitor.

Things started getting back to normal and by the end of the day I was feeling more settled. A *temp* brought my mail in to be signed as Kate was away and two of the other secretaries were off sick. One of the golden rules concerning *temps*, is to always check your post.

Peter had dictated two letters in particular which I was asked to sign in his absence. The first was to the Harrogate Magistrates' Court on behalf of a local firm who were pleading guilty by letter to a charge of overloading a vehicle. Our client's driver was in the Harrogate area when he was stopped by police and taken to a weighbridge. They discovered that the lorry was three tons overweight. Peter's letter in mitigation was perfectly written but with one small typing error. It should have read:

"We act on behalf of A.N. Other Ltd. a small haulage and scrap firm from Rotherham . . ."

Unfortunately it actually read:

"Dear Sir,

We act on behalf of A.N Other Ltd. a small haulage and crap firm from Rotherham . . ."

One wonders what the Harrogate magistrates would have thought to that but the best was saved until last. This was a letter making various representations to the Director of Public Prosecutions, an exalted officer of the legal administration. The case was one of murder, the letter one of consummate seriousness. It should have read:

> "Dear Sir,
>
> We act on behalf of AB who is due to appear before the Sheffield Crown Court on a date to be fixed
>
> We will be applying for an extension of legal aid so as to be able to instruct an expert to inspect the medical records of the deceased together with X-rays and photographs. We undertake to discharge any reasonable fees etcetera, etcetera."

Unfortunately the final sentence read:

> ". . . We undertake to discharge any reasonable fee excreta excreta."

You can imagine the reply we might have got. Peter was distraught when I told him the letter had gone unchecked. It wasn't until later that I put him out of his misery.

A week later, the *temp's* last act was to send a copy of the unaltered carbon of the letter to the Director of Public Prosecutions, as the original had got lost in the post.

At the end of the day sitting in my own office I finally

began to realise that the John Megson case was over. John and Stella were starting a new life together and the memories of the last three years of struggling for justice would begin to fade for all of us. It was maybe because it had been the best case of my career or maybe because of my age, I felt that I had to put some of those memories on paper. And so, before closing the file completely, I began to write. I had no idea that the notes that I began to jot down after the euphoria of John's release would become *Hell is not for Angels*.

XV

Hell is not for Angels: The Book

> There is an impression abroad that everyone has it in him to write one book; but if by this is implied a good book the impression is false.
>
> *W. Somerset Maugham*, The Summing Up

It was Sunday 3rd September 1995, and I was sitting in the lounge of a hotel in Dover preparing a case which was due to start the following day at the magistrates' court. It was an unusual case involving the Customs and Excise, who were claiming that my clients and others had systematically defrauded the revenue out of two million pounds of duty by reason of smuggling.

It sounds romantic, but it wasn't. I don't mind a change of scenery, but I had been in the area for over a week and Dover was closed on Sundays. I was representing seven defendants and each defendant had a set of statements and exhibits. The file ran to over fourteen thousand pieces of paper. It was a nightmare.

In my opinion it was the worst prepared case by a prosecuting authority that I had ever seen, and it was a wonder to me that a government department could get away with it, but get away with it they did. The defence were left to do all the work of putting the case and the evidence into some form of order. In the midst of all the paper, I had a copy of the Boxing News and the Sunday Times, borrowed from the hotel.

I had had enough of smuggling for one day and so I looked through the paper to see if there were any advertisements offering remedies for depression.

The headlines were uninspiring.

"Law Society say Divorce reforms are unworkable." I reminded myself of how the profession had been downgraded over the past fifteen years.

I hadn't realised that it was Harry Secombe's 74th birthday. "We are all getting old," I thought as I flicked through the announcements. I asked myself, "Who reads this stuff? You do," I replied to myself. "Ha yes but only in Dover."

"Well, well, well Salman Rushdie has been outside," I wondered if he had ever been to Dover. I think that the best way that his enemies could punish him would be to make him stay in my hotel. No one would ever think to look for him there.

I looked around me and the hotel was virtually empty. I was sitting alone in the lounge. It was raining, the bar was closed and I had to endure at least another two days of it. Why was I doing this job I wondered, what had it given me apart from ulcers and a massive overdraft? I thought that it was time to do something else. But what? No more clients, no more courts, no more dashing from town to town, no more bollockings from the magistrates and no more home work and telephone calls in the middle of the night. I was resolved to quit. Thirty years service qualified me for a gold watch, but who was going to buy it?

I returned to my newspaper and I arrived at the "Anniversaries" page to find that Johannesburg was founded in 1886 and the King of Iraq had died in 1933. All good stuff this, I thought, wondering how I could use this information in my closing speech at the end of my smuggling case.

Then it came to me, 3rd September, of course, John Megson's wedding anniversary and I had remembered the date.

I decided to contact John to see how he was. I had some spare time and it would be nice to speak to someone.

I telephoned Shaun and managed to track John down to one of his friend's houses in Llandudno in North Wales. Before signing off, I discovered that Shaun was doing reasonably well but was suffering from an old leg injury and was awaiting surgery. He tried to convince me that he was still handsome and hanging onto his remaining hair. John had kept in touch and visited him when work permitted.

I was in luck, because John was visiting his friend's house that very afternoon. I was asked to ring back.

An hour later, I rang the number again to be greeted by John who had been waiting for my call. We exchanged pleasantries and I asked for an update as to his present circumstances.

He told me that he had put the skills he had learned in prison to good use and was busy working on a large engineering contract in one of the small North Wales towns.

He was involved in re-building an ancient pier which had fallen into disrepair. He was enjoying the work, even though he worked six days a week.

More importantly, his marriage had been a success and John and Stella had settled down very well. Stella was not working, but was busy decorating their new home with a view to moving in by Christmas. I spoke to them both and they seemed extremely happy.

John explained to me how difficult it had been for him to settle down since his release from prison, but with Stella's considerable help he was managing. He had joined a local biking group who were a decent group of lads, and he was enjoying the camaraderie.

There was not a hint of bitterness concerning what he described as his lost years. He considered that he was a lucky man to be out of prison. Our conversation ended with me promising to look him up one day if I was ever in the area and he assured me that I would be made most welcome. He even offered me a ride on his motorcycle, but I declined for fear that he may try too hard to please and in doing so would frighten me half to death.

He told me that he had telephoned my office only the day before to see how I was and to use his words,

"To thank you for my first year of freedom".

I thought it a particularly nice thing to do and I was pleased that he had kept me in mind.

At the end of our call, I heard the shutters on the bar being lifted so I went to organise a drink. The waiter was a pleasant chap with dyed blonde hair and a peculiar walk. He wore a name badge which described him as *Clint*, but I doubted that was his real name.

As I sat on the stool waiting for my drink, I listened to Clint's conversation about the price of hair dye and hairdressing charges before regaining my place in the lounge where all my papers were stored.

I was relying upon every ounce of discipline I had to keep my nose to the grindstone.

After dinner I retired to bed and fell asleep while reading Rider Haggard's *Alan Quartermain.*

I was up early the next morning and I gathered all my papers together and set off for court.

The morning went well and by the time we got to lunchtime, I realised that the case against four of my clients was rather weak. I sensed that if the prosecution case did not improve, I might stand a very good chance of submitting no case and achieving some success in respect of some of my defendants. The afternoon went even better and at the close of play I was in an extremely strong position. The next morning, four of my clients were acquitted. The other three were sent to the Crown court to be dealt with, but the general result was far better than I had expected. Once again, I was to enjoy the thrill of winning a case.

On my return to the office, there was a list of telephone messages which covered the top of my desk. Why don't they telephone me when I am in, I thought to myself.

One of the telephone messages was of particular interest. It was from a woman who was concerned about her son who was serving life imprisonment for a murder that she said he had not committed. "Oh my God," I thought. "Not again," and promptly threw the message into the waste bin never wanting to see it again. I then proceeded to clear my desk.

I put all my things together, but decided to leave the office early and see if I had any garden left.

As I travelled home, I felt a strange compulsion to telephone my secretary. The conversation went something like this,

"Kate, any messages?"

"No," she said. Nothing."

"Is everything OK?" I continued.

"Yes, all quiet, your letters have been signed and have gone out in tonight's post. Is that everything?"

"Yes I think so. Oh, before you go there is one thing. Just check in my waste bin for a telephone number. It's from a woman ringing about her son. I think you had better give her a ring and invite her into the office next week."

By the summer of 1995, my notes on the Megson case had become a book and I wondered if it might be worth publishing. After spending a little time making enquiries, I was introduced to Alan Twiddle who was the business development manager of a local book publisher. We got on well and he seemed to like the book. I began to think that there were new challenges ahead for me as I got more involved in the plans for the publication of *Hell is not for Angels*.

The publication date was set for February 1996 and I was fascinated by the workings of a publishing house. I got as involved as I could with every aspect of the development of my book from typesetting and jacket design through to sales and marketing. There were one or two delays over Christmas but everything seemed set for a glittering launch in the Spring.

Then on Friday 19th January 1996 I got home from work in time to see the local news. I was shocked to see that a number of men had been arrested by the North Yorkshire Police and were to be charged with offences connected to the murder of Stephen Rowley at Scarborough Mere in 1989. I immediately realised that much of the material in my book would be regarded as *sub judice* once the men were charged. I rang Alan Twiddle who calmly said that the book would wait and that we would have an even bigger story to tell as a result. I was still incredibly disappointed that I would not be getting into print in 1996 or, knowing the speed at which the justice system can sometimes work, even 1997!

On Saturday 20th January 1996 at Scarborough Magistrates' Court, members of the Druids were charged as follows:

Animal (Colin McCombie)
Charged with the murder of Stephen Rowley.

Yettie (Simon Negrotti)
Charged with the murder of Stephen Rowley.

Snake (Brian Frankham)
Charged with violent disorder.

Geordie (George Palmer)
Charged with violent disorder.

They were all remanded in custody for six days and that evening Alan and I decided that we would put the book on hold.

On Monday 22nd January 1996 the Crown Prosecution Service rang me to let me know that at the bail application for the defendents, their solicitor had made reference to both *Rough Justice* and my book suggesting that with the amount of adverse publicity his clients had already received, there could be no chance of a fair trial.

This had prompted the prosecution to try and block this defence point by warning me that if I didn't withdraw the book, I could face a court order banning it. I did not need to be told my duties to the court, and I let them know exactly how I felt.

On Friday 26th January 1996 Geordie (George Palmer) and Snake, (Brian Frankham) were released on bail with various conditions including an order not to have any contact with any prosecution witness. Four weeks later, an application for bail by Animal (Colin McCombie) and Yettie (Simon Negrotti) was granted by a High Court judge.

On 10th April 1996, a plea and directions hearing was held at Leeds Crown Court and the matter was adjourned for a trial to take place on a date to be fixed. There were certainly a number of substantial arguments as to whether or not the defendants could get a fair trial, bearing in mind all the publicity surrounding the case. Indeed one of the defence team told me that they had decided not to apply for a court order banning the book on the basis that its publication would only reinforce their argument that a fair trial was impossible.

The local press picked up on the argument over the book and announced that it had been *BANNED* by the Crown Prosecution Service. One such article received a rebuke from the C.P.S. who denied that this had happened and demanded that their letter be printed in the offending newspaper. This was done, giving the book further publicity.

Life then quietened down again until I received a call from the defence solicitors office. They asked for a copy of the manuscript and my original case file. I refused. Later the same day they called back with the news that they had referred the matter to one of the barristers in the case who suggested that I be served with a subpoena, ordering me to produce both documents. I told the solicitor's clerk where he could put his subpoena but he did not follow my advice and issue, it he did.

XVI

The Subpoena and the Game

> "If the law supposes that," said Mr. Bumble . . .
> "The law is a ass – a idiot."
> *Charles Dickens*, "Oliver Twist"

I did not treat the service of the Subpoena lightly, although there was one amusing interlude when the enquiry agent came to serve it upon me. He had forgotten to bring any conduct money with him and for any subpoena or witness summons to be valid, the server has to deliver sufficient funds to cover the cost of travel to, and from, court. Whether he believed that solicitors could spirit themselves into court or not is another matter, but I pointed this out to him and said that in the circumstances I was unable to accept his documents. He reached into his pocket and produced a £10 note which was all the money he was carrying. I took it willingly with the words, "I'll see you in court'.

Fifteen minutes later, the enquiry agent was back telling me that he didn't have enough to get out of the car park and asking me to lend him some. I thought it was the least I could do and gave him a shiny pound coin which he readily accepted. He sheepishly asked me for another fifty pence before leaving with his tail between his legs.

The subpoena not only required me to bring to court the documents I had in relation to the appeal and the Teeside Crown Court hearings, but also my own personal documentation, including private correspondence with John and Stella. This was my private file and as such is privileged between solicitor and client.

There were three parts to my file. The first were the documents which had been sent to me by John's former solicitors, who happened to be the very same firm who were representing the defendants in this Trial. The second part were documents and statements which were served upon the Court Appeal and last but by no means least, my own personal file, including the manuscript of the book.

I took the subpoena seriously, because after all I was a solicitor of the Supreme Court and I wanted to avoid the suggestion that I was using the proceedings to publicise the book. The defence solicitors knew about the book well before I knew of any proceedings, but nevertheless I had to be careful how I dealt with their request. I decided to instruct a friend of mine called Robert Clive Smith, a barrister from Sheffield and seek his opinion on the matter. We had a consultation in which I made my various points to him and we came up with the idea of issuing a counter summons against the solicitors setting out why we considered all our documentation to be privileged. The counter summons was completed and served upon the court, the prosecution and the defence. Owing to the seriousness of the case and the importance of the matter, we decided that we would not wish to be seen to interfere with the course of justice. While we were not prepared to broadcast the manuscript, we would be prepared through our own Counsel, to let one member of the defence team read it and assure the others that there was nothing of evidential value to their case. Our point was that the book contained opinions and reflections upon the case in general and as such were not admissible as evidence.

On this basis, honour was served on both sides, but more importantly it stopped the defence from making any claim that there was material relevant to their defence which had not been handed over for scrutiny. I did not blame the defence team for acting in the way that they did, otherwise I would simply have contested the subpoena. However, publicity was to become a focal point of this case.

The trial had been fixed for Tuesday 14th January 1997, the date when we had to appear to answer the subpoena. Approximately four days before the hearing the defence notified us that we were no longer required. They had capitulated in respect of the other matters in the subpoena, obviously accepting the arguments which we had made in relation to the question of privilege.

The weeks before the trial was a worrying time for John and Stella, and indeed for the Druids, who had waited for over a year to appear before the jury. In many ways, it was asking a lot of everyone concerned to recall what had happened all those years before.

The passage of time plays cruel tricks with memory, which tends to fade after only a relatively short period. There is another old saying in the law which is, *Justice delayed is Justice denied* and in this case all the ingredients of a possible miscarriage of justice were present. There was a background of drink and drugs, defendants who were to change their stories and the lottery that a jury trial can sometimes bring about.

John and Stella had settled down to a quieter way of life and any reluctance to bring up the past must be measured against a background of fear and old habits.

John was very worried about Stella, for her health had deteriorated, and the pending ordeal of facing five senior Q.C.'s with years of experience of cross-examination and all the facts at their fingertips would have tested even the strongest witness.

I did not believe that Stella was physically and mentally equipped for what was to follow, but this did not seem to concern either defence or prosecution. I remember expressing my concerns to one of the Officers in the case but they were more concerned with the case than her welfare, something which we all had to come to terms with.

I realized that John and Stella had become pawns in a game. As a defence solicitor, I had never really given much thought to anyone other than the defendant and for the first time I was looking at a case from the witness's point of view. I confess I did not like what I was seeing. I saw the defence plotting their schemes and checking every minor detail to see if they could trip the witness up in cross-examination. I saw the prosecution considering how best to counter them. Of course, that was the job, and I have done it myself and continue to do so every day of my working life. I know that I am oblivious to anyone's welfare, except my client's and I can well understand that this is probably why so many people hate lawyers.

John and Stella entered the *game* from the minute the application in the Court of Appeal was successful. From the minute Stella made her statement to the Court of Appeal and endorsed it by giving evidence, they had both become witnesses whether they liked it or not. From then on, John and Stella were in a "no win" situation. It was true that John had his freedom, something to which he was certainly entitled but he was released into a society which appeared to be unable to either forgive or forget his conviction or indeed his membership of a fraternity who were the envy of no one except its own membership.

The Police promised to do what they could, both before and after the trial, but John feared that these were empty promises which would soon evaporate after the hearing had taken place. It was quite clear that John and Stella would lose out no matter what the outcome of these proceedings.

Having given full accounts of themselves to the Court of Appeal with their affirmations before the Teeside Crown Court, they had both become witnesses in any subsequent case and the prosecution would have issued subpoenas against them and forced them to go to court if they had refused. From the minute that Stella gave her evidence in her statement to me in Wales, she had committed herself to the action into which she was now being forced.

John too had placed himself in a difficult position and there were those who maintained that there was a moral obligation upon him to speak out. However, in the end he had no option but to give evidence.

I was amazed to see that after being a hero upon his release, he was turned into a villain by some because of the circumstances which had been forced upon him. A number of people even believed that he should have stayed in custody and served the life sentence.

I was satisfied that John had paid his dues and more but what of Stella? In any version of the events, she had inflicted no wounds. She had not helped or encouraged the savage attack that had taken Stephen Rowley's young life. However while giving evidence and later, she was made to feel that she was in some way responsible.

Shortly before the trial, John complained of a number of bikers who he didn't recognise, visiting his local public house and having more than a passing interest in the regular customers. He saw this as an example of witness intimidation and he would report many other worrying incidents in the days leading up to the trial. He explained that he was not worried for himself but Stella who had two children and her health which was not good at the best of times, was not improved by the extra worry brought on by these events.

The police eventually took John's concern seriously and moved them into a safe house for the period of the trial. Another incident in which a young woman resembling Stella was attacked and stabbed just a short distance from Stella's home seemed to reinforce John's very real concern.

XVII

The Final Trial and the Verdict

> Judgment for an evil thing is many times delayed some day or two, some century or two, but it is sure as life, it is sure as death.
>
> *Thomas Carlyle*

The combined effect of the *Rough Justice* exposures, considerable media attention and, most importantly, the new evidence brought out at John's successful appeal was to persuade the police and Prosecuting authorities to reopen their investigations and look at the case afresh. It seemed clear that the person or persons directly responsible for inflicting the fatal wounds on that fateful night at Scarborough Mere remained at large and unpunished.

Attention now focused upon the members of the Druids who, with Megson, had stumbled down the hill and through the trees to Rowley's camp. Their collective denials of any involvement in the murder, which they gave during the 1989 interviews, lay in tatters. And so, in 1995 the police called them in for further questioning.

Eight years after the event, and six years after John's original conviction for murder, four more members of the Druids attended at Leeds Crown Court to stand trial for offences connected with the tragic events at Scarborough. Animal (Colin McCombie) and Yettie (Simon Negrotti) were charged with murder, while Snake (Brian Frankham) and Geordie (George Palmer) stood accused of violent disorder.

The hearing began in Court Five on 14th January 1997 before the presiding High Court Judge Mr Justice Poole. The Prosecution, led by an experienced and able silk, Robert Smith Q.C. from Leeds, proceeded to present the evidence against the accused, which included crucial testimony from John and Stella. Stella was taken into protective custody for the duration of her evidence but it must have been an ordeal for her to face at least four of Her Majesty's Queen's Counsel over a period of two to three days in the witness box.

Her attention span was effected by her illness, let alone the trauma of giving evidence and appearing in front of the defendants. Nevertheless Stella gave her evidence, sticking to her guns on the salient points, but she was subject to much criticism by the defence. The weekend intervened to interrupt Stella's evidence and she told me afterwards of the great strain this had imposed upon her. As anticipated, the various Counsel for the defendants vigorously attacked her account. To a very great extent, the cases against the four in the dock depended upon Stella convincing the judge and jury of what she claimed to have seen. Unfortunately for the prosecution, there was no corroboration of what Stella had seen, and this substantially weakened the prosecution case.

The following week John was in the witness box giving his evidence much in line with his statement to the police and indeed his original letter to the *Rough Justice* team. There was an argument to say that he still complied with his Biker's Code, for in his evidence he said that he did not see who stabbed Stephen Rowley.

He was cross-examined about this book and about the suggestion that a film company were interested in the film rights. John knew nothing of either proposition. When I became aware that a case was ongoing, I withdrew the book and took no further steps with it, except to discuss the idea with a film company in London. I had spoken to them a considerable time before, but had explained that the sub judice rules prevented publication.

Again, the defence had seized upon this and suggested to John that he had a financial motive for giving evidence. The constant references to publication of materials concerning the case had led the judge to impose a *gagging order* upon the press and television, with the result that there was a limitation upon what material could be published. This order was maintained throughout the trial, and I believe was used to stop the defence having grounds to complain that the trial was not proceeding fairly.

After John's evidence had been completed, Josephine was called to give evidence by the prosecution but I could not understand their reason for calling her. It was possibly a way to stop the defence from using her, but as she would be available for cross-examination, any points that the defence thought were appropriate, could then be made. She had changed her ground somewhat from her original statements to the police, and accepted that she was present with Stella on the night, at or about the scene of the murder. She had previously denied being there, but now told the jury that she was a distance behind Stella and couldn't see anything of the incident. She was unsure what had taken place, but at least her evidence did place

Stella at the scene and to that extent Stella's evidence was corroborated, something which had not been available to the Court of Appeal.

At the end of the prosecution case, certain legal arguments were made and the judge ruled in accordance with the defence submissions that the basis of evidence against McCombie and Negrotti was insufficient to warrant the charges of murder being put to the jury. The jury were therefore instructed to consider charges of manslaughter against the two men.

Not one of the four defendants chose to enter the witness box to give his account of the events in open court. This avoided any possible revealing cross-examination from the prosecution. The only explanations for the night's events were contained in the records of their interviews from the Autumn of 1995, and these were duly read out to the court.

Throughout the interview, despite several hours of police probing, little light was shed on the events which had happened over six years before. No-one accepted responsibility for the stabbing and no-one identified the true culprit.

McCombie's reaction to the questioning was reticent and somewhat timorous. He appeared weary of the matter and many of his responses, especially in the last few interviews, were laced with dry sarcasm. His most noteworthy utterance, and the one to which the judge drew the jury's particular attention in his summing up of the evidence, was a matter-of-fact acceptance that it was in the minds of all who traipsed down to Rowley's encampment in the dead of night that a fight would take place. Violence was clearly anticipated and intended.

Negrotti explained that his purpose in following the

group had been to exert some control over Megson and escort him back to their camp before he could cause any harm. He was also at pains to emphasise that the attack had taken place in the early hours when it was dark and there was a mist shrouding the mere. In other words, Negrotti had seen nothing.

At one point in his interview he remembered that a lifeless form had fallen on his foot, which he had proceeded to push away in the direction of the prostrate Megson. He had kicked no-one but he was aware that others had been involved in an assault, although he was unable to name anyone. His final act had been to drag Megson from beneath the limp and motionless body.

It was alleged by Negrotti that Stella had been *off her head* on Acid, and he recalled ushering her and Josephine away from the scene, though he was muted and equivocal as to whether he had told them that someone had been stabbed. He stated that he may have said something *bad* had happened and may have admitted to a sense of unease that matters had got out of hand. He knew that there had been kicking by others, and he feared that knives may have been used.

Negrotti claimed that at the time of his original interrogation in 1989 he had shown the police a key ring knife which he told them belonged to Stella Harris. Stella denied this and the police believed that any such exhibit would have been recorded at the time on Negrotti's record of detention.

Continuing the tenor of McCombie and Negrotti's threadbare accounts, Frankham suggested that the notion of confrontation had been instigated by Megson who, according to Frankham, had been fired up in a *vodka frenzy*. He stated that members of the party had tried to prevent Megson going down to Rowley's camp but, failing in this, had followed him with the implicit intention of soothing his reckless spirit and restoring calm.

Frankham claimed that the assault had taken place without his direct participation and had finished by the time he approached the tent. Again, the police attempts during interviews with Frankham to uncover the guilty party were met with silence. Frankham had not seen, did not know and could not say anything.

As the events of the Rowley encampment unfolded, Frankham was preoccupied ensuring that Rowley's companions in the car, which was a short distance up the hill, did not get out and join the fray. This action, he would have the police believe, was motivated by a protective benevolence. He accepted, the police allegation that he had approached the car wielding a stick, but protested that, rather than using it in a threatening manner, he needed it as a walking aid, due to leg injuries he had suffered in a recent motor cycle accident. He acknowledged that he had spoken to the youths, but denied that he had been threateningly malevolent. He said that his intention was to reduce the chances of more people becoming involved in the brawl, which would have inevitably caused an escalation of violence. He refuted that his tone had been aggressive, but he conceded that there may have been a note of urgency or desperation in his advice to the teenagers to stay put and not get involved in the one-sided battle below.

Frankham said that his involvement in the events ended when he walked Stella and Jo back to the Druids' camp. It was not until later that morning, following the arrival of the police, that he first became aware that anyone had been stabbed. He had gone to bed thinking that there had merely been a *kicking*.

When asked about his visit to Wales, he denied that his reason had been to pressurise Stella into retracting her statement. He asserted that his real intention had been to uncover the truth behind rumours that the *Outlaws* biker gang had plans to break up the Druids gang.

Of all the interviews recorded in the autumn of 1995, Geordie (George Palmer) gave the most forthright and full account, despite the fact that he claimed to play a very minor role. He gave the same account of events as in the others' interviews, generally suggesting that whatever happened had been instigated by a brazen Megson while pouring scorn on the correctness and credibility of Stella's evidence. As with the other defendants before him, he was wholly unable to identify who had done what to whom.

His version of the story began when he had been awoken and told by one of the girls that some of the Druids had gone *to give someone a hiding*. Making his own way, he followed the trail down to Rowley's base, with the sole intention of ensuring everything was OK. Although he admitted he was completely drunk, as far as he was aware, no-one followed him.

Standing within four to five yards of the tent, Palmer saw Rowley emerge from its partially collapsed interior and begin to hit Megson. At this point, the Druids, who were stood around, converged on the youth and his friend, Darren Lynne who had by now, had the misfortune to clamber from beneath the canvas and join him. Palmer claimed that he was unable to discern anything definite from the confused melee in front of him, as he was still half asleep and completely drunk.

His attention was then drawn to the car parked behind him further up the slope. The vehicle's headlights had come on and illuminated the group round the tent. Seeing the occupants of the car awake, and preparing to get out, Palmer walked towards it with Frankham, who had moved away from the group around Rowley.

Palmer denied having a stick, or even seeing anyone with one. He also denied saying anything to either of the youths in the car but he remembered that one had gone so far as to put one of this feet out of the door before being warned by Frankham to the effect that he had better stay put unless he *wanted some*.

Palmer accepted that he was ready to fight if he had to and that, had the occupants got out of the car, he would have confronted them. He went even further, suggesting that had it been necessary, he would have thrown his weight into the fray around the tent. However, he pointed out that this was hardly necessary as the Druids appeared to have the upper hand.

Although he was unable to shed any light upon what had happened around the tent, Palmer spoke of having heard muffled moans and groans, and at one stage, he thought he had heard someone shout, "He's been stabbed!"

He criticised Stella's portrayal of events on the basis that she had not been there, and that even if she had, from where she said she was there would have been nothing she could have seen through the early morning gloom.

Palmer accepted that earlier in the evening he and others had made comments suggesting that the teenagers down the slope deserved a *good kicking* for their annoying behaviour, but he stressed that was as far as he would have gone.

Referring to the meeting at the clubhouse the day after the stabbing, Palmer had forgotten most of what went on, except that Megson had been unwilling to accept and admit responsibility for the killing.

Palmer's explanation of his excursion to Wales with Frankham differed to that of his co-accused. His reason for going had been to discover what the *Rough Justice* programme contained.

Despite the Druids' initial denial of any involvement, Megson's appeal had forced them to acknowledge that they had been down to Rowley's camp, and, in the cases of McCombie and Negrotti, to accept that they had been stood around the tent in the immediate vicinity of Rowley, when the fateful blows had been struck.

When the jury went out they spent the whole day deliberating on their verdicts. They were not agreed and the following morning the judge gave the majority verdict directions. A jury must find when reaching its verdict that they are unanimous, but there comes a time after many hours of deliberations when the law provides that a jury can return a verdict of not less than ten to two and this process is called a majority verdict.

It was not until after lunch on the second day that the jury were finally agreed by a majority of ten to two.

The jury returned to Court Five, and as ever in jury trials the adrenaline was flowing, but there was complete silence as the foreman of the jury stood to give his verdicts.

The clerk of the court asked the foreman if the jury had achieved a verdict upon which not less than ten of them were agreed, and the foreman answered, "Yes".

McCombie was the first to be dealt with,

"How do you find the defendant Colin John

McCombie. Guilty or not guilty of manslaughter?"

Almost, as if in slow motion, the proceedings began and the foreman of the jury announced,

"Guilty."

"Mr Foreman, has the jury reached a verdict upon not less than ten of you are agreed in respect of Simon John Negrotti?"

"Yes."

"What is your verdict?" asked the court clerk "Do you find the defendant Simon John Negrotti guilty or not guilty of manslaughter?"

"Guilty," came the reply and there were gasps from the public gallery.

The court clerk then directed her attention to Brian Frankham.

"Members of the jury in the case of Brian Frankham, have you reached a verdict upon which not less than ten of you are agreed?"

"Yes," said the foreman.

"Then," said the court clerk, "How do you find the defendant Brian Frankham on the count of violent disorder. Guilty or not guilty?"

"Not guilty," replied the foreman and Brian Frankham took a deep breath and hung his head.

The court clerk then turned her attention to George Palmer and the same questions were asked.

Palmer stared at the foreman of the jury, as if transfixed by the events which were surrounding him.

"How do you find the defendant George Palmer?" said the court clerk "Guilty or not guilty of violent disorder?"

"Not guilty," said the foreman of the jury, equally as firmly as before and Palmer nodded, seemingly in agreement.

Counsel for Frankham and Palmer asked that their respective clients be released from the dock, and the judge simply replied "Let them be released" and they left without a word to anyone.

McCombie and Negrotti remained standing in the dock showing silent but defiant disapproval of the jury's verdict.

The case against McCombie and Negrotti was adjourned in order that the court could have the benefit of a probation officers report which would give an insight into the defendants' backgrounds and perhaps assist the court in arriving at a decision as to sentence.

It was going to be an extremely interesting exercise to see how the judge dealt with that particular question because John had been sentenced to seven years imprisonment on the basis of manslaughter and the rules of parity would seem to decree that the other defendants should be dealt with in the same way.

This raised a particular point because Mr Justice McPherson at Teeside had specifically asked what sentence he would have to impose to enable John to be released immediately.

We had worked out that seven years would be appropriate, and indeed any less might mean that he had served more than he should.

It was a point which we were to ponder for the next four weeks leading up to sentence.

Remarkably, there appeared to be little jubilation in the released defendants camp and when Frankham and Palmer were released both Yorkshire Television and BBC were refused interviews.

I was notified of the result by David Clarke, the reporter for the Sheffield Star who had been covering the story throughout the trial. He asked me if I had any comment to make and I indicated that my thoughts were with Stephen Rowley's family while expressing relief that the matter was over.

I had no other feelings as my job was simply to represent John Megson and to try to bring about his release. I undertook that task as any solicitor would, just as the Druid's solicitor's had approached their representation at the trial.

As we went about our business for the day and prepared for the cases which were to occupy our interests in the forthcoming weeks, McCombie and Negrotti set about beginning the sentence which was to be imposed four weeks later. The only question was, how long? But only Mr Justice Poole knew the answer.

The day after the verdict, YTV released a report on the story together with an interview with John and me. There had been a certain amount of media coverage during the trial until the judge had actually stopped it, but it was sufficient to remind the public just who John was. The down side was the notoriety that the publicity was to impose upon John. I arranged to meet him shortly before McCombie and Negrotti were sentenced and the venue was a pub just outside Sheffield. I felt distinctly out of place in my collar and tie, and when I entered I was viewed with great suspicion by an array of rather fearsome clientele. I asked John if it was his local and was amused to be told that he had never been there before. We stayed for ten minutes or so and then beat a hasty retreat to a quieter venue.

I was keen to hear his views on the case and more importantly how he saw his future. He expressed no interest in the book or in any of the publicity that had been afforded to it. I thought at least he might be interested in the talk of a film, but he wasn't.

It was interesting to note that his main concern was for Stella and also the Rowley family, something which he had dealt with at some depth on the television interview, but owing to the pressures of time much of it had been edited out.

His main problem was that he was unemployed. He described how his last employer was unaware of exactly who he was, but when he saw John on a news item on television, he *dispensed with his services*.

I was surprised that this would happen, because the television programmes and the various items about him had not been uncomplimentary and indeed I thought that the publicity might stand him in good stead, but it appears that I was wrong. His other difficulty was that certain members of the biker fraternity, despite their earlier support, had shown disapproval of John giving evidence at Leeds Crown Court.

I could not help observing that there would be no queue to occupy John's position, certainly if he had served out the remainder of his life sentence. Nevertheless, John saw his biking career as being over, and with Stella's health slowly deteriorating, John had begun to feel more and more isolated.

His other concern was that in the eyes of the court, he had not fully managed to establish that he was not the stabber of Stephen Rowley. Quite how anyone could possibly imagine that he would have been responsible for all the injuries to Rowley and to Darren Lynn and the threats to Drakesmith in the car, and also to be in the form of more than one biker, defeats reason.

For the whole of the month prior to sentencing, the

Bikers Story was at the forefront of my mind and everywhere I went, people began to ask the question,

"Who really did kill Stephen Rowley?"

I began to wonder whether anyone had really been listening at all.

The sentencing date had not been fixed, but I was most interested in how the judge would sentence McCombie and Negrotti, and the basis upon which he was to do it.

For the next few weeks we waited with baited breath.

The day arrived, and His Honour Mr Justice Poole sentenced both McCombie and Negrotti to six years' imprisonment. He outlined the events for a final time. He considered there had been drinking and boisterous behaviour from all who had attended the Mere that weekend, most of whom were young and in holiday mood. There was a disturbance caused by three youths speeding in their car, at least some of whom he thought probably were members of Rowley's contingent, though no harm had been caused. As dusk fell, there was a good deal of shouting between different camp sites, including intermittent abuse between the Druids and the youngsters further down the slope.

By 2 am, night had settled and quiet enclosed the camp. A decision had been taken at the Druid's site, to which Megson, McCombie and Negrotti were all a party, to steal down to Rowley's encampment on what the judge characterised a *punitive expedition*, there to inflict terror and violence upon the sleeping teenagers who had unwittingly caused such offence.

The judge thought there to be insufficient evidence to establish that either McCombie or Negrotti had been aware before, or during the assault that knives were to be or were being used, though he considered that

Negrotti at least had realized in the immediate aftermath that this had been the case.

Stephen Rowley's death had occurred in the context of the group's decision to inflict terror and violence, a decision to which both had consented and gone out of their way to pursue.

The Judge summarised that Rowley had emerged from his collapsed tent and, confronted by the bulk of Megson, proceeded to lash out towards him, whereupon he had been attacked. He rejected Negrotti's account of how he had used his feet merely to push collapsed bodies away from him, and considered it very possible that he had participated in the kicking.

The judge claimed that neither defendant had shown any real remorse for the tragic outcome of their collective assault.

Beyond this inexact appraisal, the judge felt it was impossible to do any more than speculate. He made explicit and condemnatory reference to the *wall of silence* erected by the biker gang, of which eight years expensive investigation, examination and trials had failed to do more than dislodge the *odd brick*.

The truth may lurk still behind its confines. Or it may be that, as Defence Counsel for Negrotti and McCombie said to Megson in his cross-examination:

"Fact, fantasy, half-truths and lies have become indistinguishable to the parties, tangled in the vines of their own deceit. Maybe the lapse of time, dimness of the night, extent of most of the group's inebriation and inevitable confusion of a melee have all conspired to smudge a picture none of the participants seem willing to paint."

The Judge concluded by saying that it was unlikely that

anyone would know exactly what happened on that fateful night in April 1989. With all due respect, I disagree: the facts speak for themselves. The difficulty with trials is that the full picture does not always present itself, and sometimes it cannot do so because of the legal constraints which are put upon what evidence can be admitted and what cannot. It is a matter for speculation as to what the jury would have thought had they heard the forensic evidence which we used in the build up to the hearing at Teeside. The jury may also have felt differently if there had been corroboration of Stella's statement and indeed, if they had been informed of Stella's health, which may or may not have explained her demeanour in the witness box.

There is an old saying in South Yorkshire: *The jungle drums are never wrong*; but in this case the judge and jury never heard them.

Epilogue

> It hurts that I have been with these people for a lot of years and I trusted them with my life. We go out to a race meeting, and then this happens . . .
>
> I'm just happy I'm nothing to do with these people any more, and that people know now that I'm not the one who stabbed him.
>
> *John Megson*
> *Rough Justice: The Biker's Tale*
> *1994*

Almost exactly eight years after the enquiry into the murder of Stephen Rowley had begun, the third set of proceedings had ended. Three men stood convicted of manslaughter, John Megson in 1994 and Colin McCombie and Simon Negrotti in 1997.

This case highlighted how juries and those connected with the legal system suffer from the frailties of the human condition. How was it that the Court of Appeal could have one view of the case and the crown court at Leeds another, with each giving different opinions based upon essentially similar evidence? Tragically, as with many decisions in life it came down to how people reacted in court on the day.

Despite my thirty years in the profession, I will never understand how juries think.

After the final trial John told me that the law was nothing more than a lottery. He said that his ticket number had come up once and it was unlikely that it would ever reappear.

Dealing with both the unfortunates of this world and the most devious of clients I have always tried my very best to represent them fairly. Their victims may feel that they are unworthy of any representation whether paid for by the legal aid system or not. However, in a television interview John gave after his release, when asked about Stephen Rowley, he said, "What must his family be thinking?'. I could not answer this question and it is one that I have never dared to ask because Rowley's family are indeed the true victims in this case. When in 1994/95 I was fighting for Megson and when the other bikers, solicitors and Counsel were fighting for them in 1996/97, there was little time to think of the victims. We all had a job to do and a duty to protect our clients' rights. If this is seen to be unfair or unreasonable there would be no legal representation for defendants at all and this would lead to anarchy. However, this is no comfort to those who have suffered as a result of crime.

How fair the system is, depends from which side it is being seen at any one time.

The decision of the Court of Appeal in 1995 and subsequently the Teeside Crown Court accepted that John Megson was not responsible for the stabbing. Indeed he only admitted his part in the affair on the understanding that the records shows that he was not the stabber. Cynically it could be suggested that they have all got away with it but however strongly they protest they will all carry the blood of Stephen Rowley on their hands. The other bikers claimed that the decision of the jury in 1997 confirmed that they were not the stabbers of Stephen Rowley.

The Stephen Rowley case was an intriguing story of loyalty and disloyalty, of truth and lies, honour and dishonour and in the end, the system was unable to either accept or confirm the truth.

As time passes many theories and speculations will come to light and indeed the convicted men have already lodged appeals and lawyers believe that due to a number of legal technicalities there is every chance that the appeals will be successful.

Both John and Stella were praised following John's release. John for his loyalty, however misplaced, to his former friends and Stella for her bravery in coming forward to tell the truth about what she had seen. Now it seems they are being vilified by the same people for merely repeating the evidence they had given to the Court of Appeal. After the trial there was even a suggestion of a conspiracy between John and Stella to secure John's release. Since being freed at Teeside, John and Stella had become public property as far as the case was concerned and they had no alternative but to confirm the case as set before the Court of Appeal. They would have been criticised had they not done so and indeed may well have found themselves in trouble with the courts. It is therefore understandable why potential witnesses in criminal cases refuse to make statements and become involved. Although an individual owes a duty to the court and the public at large there is an argument which says that we have a duty to ourselves. The British Government has recognised the increasing level of the intimidation of witnesses and has placed a new offence of witness intimidation on the statute books. However it is a charge that is difficult to prove and affords no real protection until after the event. There simply is not the facility to protect witnesses twenty four hours a day by a police force which is already bursting at the seams dealing with bureaucracy.

The only certainty, after all the time and money that has been spent taking the case through the institutions of justice, is that no-one stands convicted of the murder of Stephen Rowley.

I am often asked about the *Biker case* and I find that I now try to be as diplomatic as I can.

When I accepted John Megson's case, I accepted that he was innocent of the charge of murder. I believed that British justice would right the wrong and I pursued an ideal which was bound to fall short of perfection. Today when I am asked who really did kill Stephen Rowley my answer has become: "I can tell you who didn't do it" the rest depends on what you want to believe.

Has our legal system failed us? History tells us that it has happened before and I know that it will happen again. We must all live in hope that it never happens to us.